AWESOME LEGO CREATIONS

with Bricks You Already Have

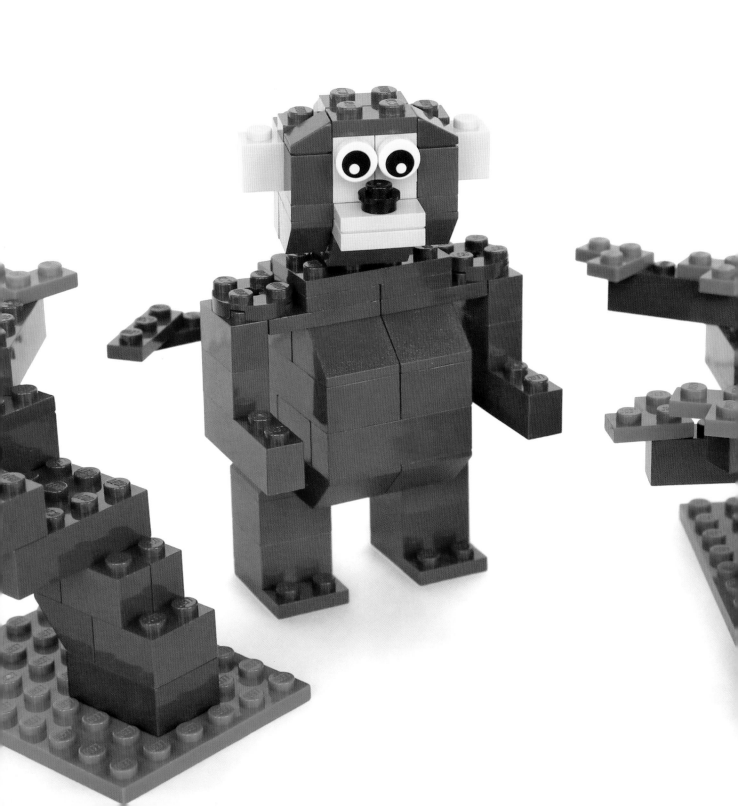

AWESOME LEGO CREATIONS

with Bricks You Already Have

50 New Robots, Dragons, Race Cars, Planes, Wild Animals
and Other Exciting Projects to Build Imaginative Worlds

SARAH DEES
founder of Frugal Fun for Boys

PAGE STREET
PUBLISHING CO.

PAGE STREET
PUBLISHING CO.

First published in 2016 by
Page Street Publishing Co.
27 Congress Street, Suite 105
Salem, MA 01970
www.pagestreetpublishing.com

Distributed by Macmillan, sales in Canada by The Canadian Manda Group.

LEGO, the Brick and Knob configurations and the Minifigure are trademarks of the LEGO Group, which does not sponsor, authorize or endorse this book.

21   20   19   18   8   9   10   11

ISBN-13: 978-1-62414-281-9
ISBN-10: 1-62414-281-8

Library of Congress Control Number: 2016936934

Cover and book design by Page Street Publishing Co.
Photography by Sarah Dees

Printed and bound in China

DEDICATION

To Jordan and our wonderful children—Aidan, Gresham, Owen, Jonathan and Janie. This book was truly a family endeavor from dreaming up the ideas to designing the projects and counting all the bricks, and I couldn't have done it without all of you! Also to my brother Andy, who was my first LEGO building companion.

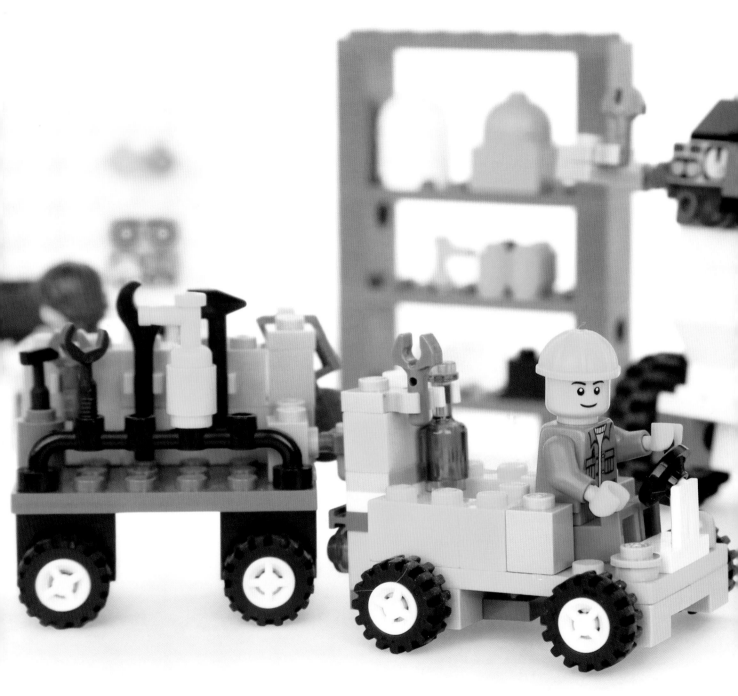

CONTENTS

HOW TO USE THIS BOOK

A day without LEGO is like a day without sunshine! At least, that is the opinion at our house. We love building with LEGO and we love sharing our ideas. We want you to think of this book as a creative guide that will spark new ideas in your own imagination.

This book contains two types of LEGO projects: Step-by-Step and No-Instruction Creative Challenge.

We have included step-by-step instructions for many of the projects because we have found that it can be frustrating to try to copy a design without being able to see which bricks were used. These projects begin with a detailed parts list to assist you in finding all of the pieces you will need.

The No-Instruction Creative Challenge projects are simple to build from the pictures or are more open-ended and imaginative in nature. They are designed to inspire your own building and it is not necessary to use the exact bricks we used. These projects begin with a key elements list which specifies the pieces that are essential for making the project work the way it is pictured and then you can get creative with your own bricks from there.

For any of the projects, don't feel limited by the colors and bricks that we chose! If you don't have the exact parts needed for a project, make substitutions with your own bricks. You may even discover an improvement that makes the project look better!

It's definitely possible that you will find a project in this book that you want to build but don't have all of the bricks needed. It's always good to get creative and make substitutions. If you really want it to look like the project in the book, however, it's not very difficult or expensive to get your hands on individual LEGO bricks.

There are basically two options for ordering bricks and both will require help from your parents. One is to order from the Pick-A-Brick section on lego.com and the other is to order from a third party LEGO seller. You might not be aware of this, but every LEGO brick has a tiny ID number on it, usually on the underside. This ID number is specific to that part but not specific to the color. So if you put that number in the search bar on lego.com's Pick-A-Brick page, you will be able to see all of the colors available for that brick. Then you can order the one that you need. However, note that orders from Pick-A-Brick ship from Denmark and it can take a long time to receive your order. We have had orders take up to one month to arrive.

Another option is to order from http://bricklink.com. Brick Link is a site that hosts many different sellers of LEGO bricks and you can also purchase unopened sets and custom sets. The prices on Brick Link are related to supply and demand, meaning that a basic brick in a common color will cost very little while a hard-to-find collectible minifigure will sell for much more. Each vendor on Brick Link charges for shipping separately, so be aware of this when adding bricks to your cart. If you buy 8 different parts from 8 different vendors, you are going to pay 8 different shipping fees! What seems to work well is to look for a vendor with a high feedback number next to their name. If they have a lot of feedback, they have completed a lot of transactions and that means that they probably have a lot of bricks to offer. It's more likely that you will be able to find several bricks that you need from the same high volume vendor and you can save on shipping.

LEGO bricks come in many different colors. The colors are listed on the Pick-A-Brick section of lego.com and the Brick Link site also includes a color guide. Because Brick Link vendors sell both new and used LEGO bricks, they have a system of color names that includes older colors that have now been discontinued. For example, the current light gray and dark gray bricks are referred to as light bluish gray and dark bluish gray on Brick Link.

Be sure to clear any purchases with Mom or Dad and get their help when using websites like Brick Link or the official LEGO site!

Have fun creating new worlds with your LEGO bricks!

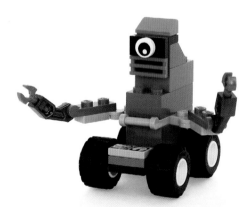

BRICK GUIDE

Did you know that LEGO bricks have names? Putting together LEGO sets does not require a person to know the names of the bricks used. But what happens if you want to order individual bricks online? In this brick guide, you will find the names of many of the bricks that we have used in this book. This is not an exhaustive list of all of the LEGO bricks available, but this guide will help you to understand the terms used in the parts lists for each project and to find individual bricks when ordering online.

There are differences in the names of bricks depending on whether you are ordering from Lego.com's Pick-A-Brick site or from a third party LEGO vendor such as Brick Link (http://bricklink.com). Throughout the book, the names on Brick Link are used more often as it is an easier site from which to order.

Keep in mind also that any LEGO brick can be easily located on Pick-A-Brick (http://lego.com) by searching the ID number on the brick. This tiny number is usually on the underside of the brick.

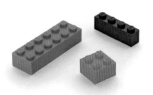

BRICKS

These are bricks. Count the number of dots (studs) to determine the brick's size. The red brick is a 2 x 2, for example, because it has two studs on each side.

MODIFIED BRICKS

These are bricks that are modified in some way. Pick-A-Brick calls them "bricks, special," and Brick Link calls them "bricks, modified." Bricks can be modified with an axle, a handle, a clip, a stud on the side and more. The green brick is a headlight. Notice that there is a small notch in the bottom front of the brick, while the yellow brick is smooth except for the stud. In this book, we have used these two bricks interchangeably.

ROUND BRICKS

The light blue brick is a 1 x 1, the red is a 2 x 2 and the dark gray is a 4 x 4.

PLATES

Both Pick-A-Brick and Brick Link use the word plates for these bricks. The dark gray brick is a 4 x 4 round plate. The black plate is a wedge. A wedge plate is any plate that has a triangular shape. This particular wedge plate is a corner and the sides are equal. The type of wedge plates used for airplane wings have one longer side and either a right or left orientation.

MODIFIED PLATES

These bricks are called "plates, special" on Pick-A-Brick and "plates, modified" on Brick Link. Plates can be modified to have one stud on top, a clip on the end or clips on the side, a handle on the end or on the side, etc.

SLOPE BRICKS

As you can tell from the shape, these are slope bricks. They are organized under "bricks, sloping" on Pick-A-Brick. However, Pick-A-Brick refers to bricks such as the red 2 x 2 and the gray 2 x 3 as roof tiles and Brick Link refers to them as slope bricks. The brown 2 x 2 brick is a slope, inverted. The red 1 x 3 is a curved slope. The blue brick is a 1 x 1 slope, 30 degree (Brick Link). Some projects use a brick that is a 1 x 2 slope, 45 degree triple, which means it's a 45-degree slope with three sides.

BRACKETS

These bricks are called brackets (Brick Link) or angle plates (Pick-A-Brick). Brackets are very useful for building on the side. Either site refers to the size in both dimensions. For example, the blue bracket is a 1 x 2—1 x 4. The light gray bracket is considered inverted.

CONES AND DOMES

The red and brown bricks are cones and the orange brick is a 2 x 2 round dome.

TILES

Plate bricks that are smooth on the top are called tiles. Pick-A-Brick refers to them as flat tiles, while on Brick Link they are tiles. The small light gray brick is a panel (Brick Link) or a wall element (Pick-a-Brick).

TECHNIC BRICKS

The bricks shown in this photo are referred to as Technic bricks even though they also come in many sets that are not Technic sets. Bricks with holes are Technic Bricks. The white brick is a liftarm (Brick Link). Technic axles have an x shape. Some have a stop on the end and others do not. They are measured by the number of studs long.

CHAPTER 1

ROBOT LAB

LEGO robots are fun to build because they can either be technical looking or fun and full of personality. These LEGO robots have a little of both! Once you have assembled your robots, build a lab for them complete with minifigure scientists. There is always something interesting happening at the robot lab!

SIMON THE MECHANICAL ROBOT
STEP-BY-STEP

This three-wheeled robot can zip quickly around the lab as he delivers tools to the scientists and performs repairs on the machines. He has buttons on the front of his body that can be used to program him for all sorts of tasks. A turntable brick allows his head to spin all the way around and his arms are posable.

PARTS LIST

LIGHT GRAY BRICKS
1—2 x 2 plate
1—1 x 2 plate
1—1 x 4 plate
2—1 x 3 plates
2—1 x 2 plates with a clip on the end
1—1 x 1 plate with clip
1—2 x 3 wedge plate, right
1—2 x 3 wedge plate, left
4—1 x 2 bricks
1—2 x 4 brick
2—1 x 1 bricks with a stud on the side
2—2 x 2 slopes, inverted
4—1 x 2 slopes, inverted
2—1 x 2 slopes, 30 degree
1—bracket 2 x 2—1 x 2
2—antennas
4—technic connector pins

DARK GRAY BRICKS
2—1 x 1 plates with a clip light (round hole)
1—2 x 6 plate
2—1 x 2 plates with pin
2—1 x 2 plates with a handle on the end
2—1 x 2 pin connector plates with two holes
1—2 x 4 brick
2—1 x 2 bricks with ridges
2—brackets 2 x 2—2 x 1
2—1 x 2 Technic bricks
2—1 x 4 Technic bricks
2—1 x 1 round tiles
1—1 x 1 gauge tile
1—2 x 1 gauge tile

BLACK BRICKS
2—2 x 4 plates
3—2 x 2 plates
2—1 x 4 plates

1—1 x 6 plate
2—3 x 3 wedge plates, corner
8—1 x 2 bricks
1—2 x 4 brick
1—2 x 2 brick
3—2 x 2 slopes
3—wheels
2—pins
1—wrench

WHITE BRICKS
2—1 x 2 plates
1—2 x 2 plate, turntable
1—1 x 6 plate
9—2 x 4 bricks
1—1 x 4 brick
2—1 x 2 bricks
2—2 x 2 bricks
3—2 x 2 slopes, inverted
2—eyes

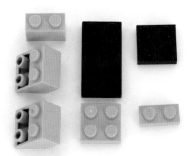

STEP 1: Gather the pieces shown for the head.

STEP 2: Start with the 2 x 2 light gray plate on the bottom. Add the two 2 x 2 inverted slopes, then the 2 x 4 black plate. The top layer is a 1 x 2 light gray plate, a 1 x 2 light gray brick and a 2 x 2 black plate.

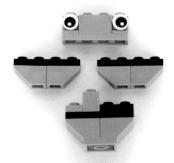

STEP 3: Build the eyes and the right and left sides of the face as shown. Each eye is attached to a 1 x 1 brick with a stud on the side.

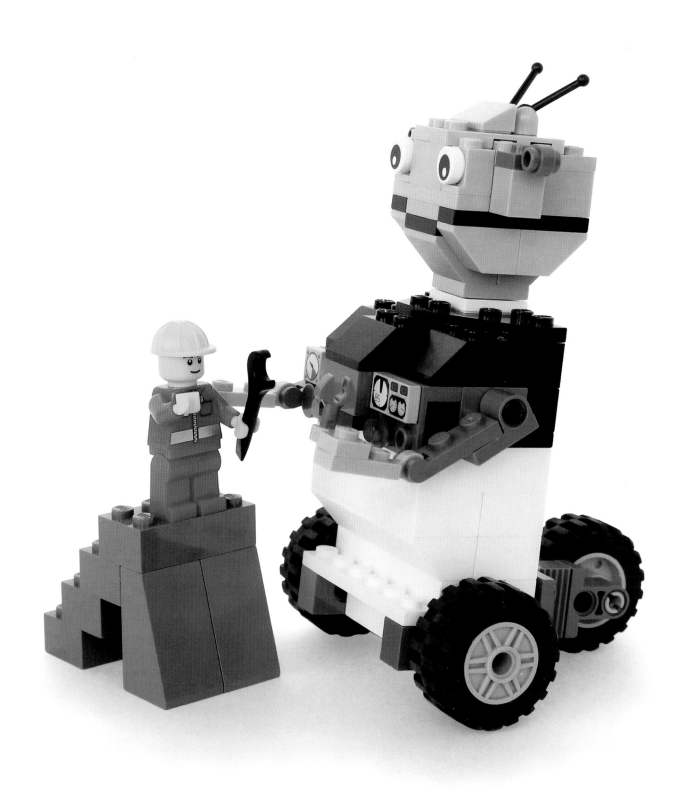

 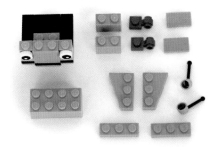 

STEP 4: Attach the three sections of the face to the underside of the eyes as shown.

STEP 5: The pieces shown will be needed to build the rest of the head.

STEP 6: Add the 2 x 4 brick and two 1 x 2 bricks to the head.

 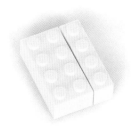 

STEP 7: Complete the head. First, place one 1 x 3 plate (regular, not the wedge plates) on each side of the head just behind the eyes. Then add the rest of the pieces as shown.

STEP 8: Build the body. Start with a 2 x 4 white brick and a 1 x 4 white brick.

STEP 9: Add two 1 x 2 white plates and place a light gray bracket 1 x 2—2 x 2 on top of that.

 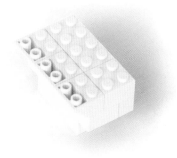 

STEP 10: Fill in with white bricks around the gray bracket.

STEP 11: Add three 2 x 2 inverted slopes, a 2 x 4 brick and a 2 x 2 brick. Make sure that the inverted slopes face the opposite side of the body as the gray bracket.

STEP 12: Build up the body by adding two layers of 2 x 4 white bricks.

STEP 13: Add a black 2 x 4 plate to the middle of the robot's body and make sure that it hangs over the edge by one stud (as shown). Place a 1 x 2 black brick on either side of the 2 x 4 plate and then add two 2 x 2 plates and a 1 x 6 plate.

STEP 14: Build up the body as shown. The Technic bricks will hold the arms on each side of the robot.

STEP 15: Add two dark gray brackets 1 x 2— 2 x 2 to the front of the robot.

STEP 16: Use black bricks, three of them slopes, to finish up the body.

STEP 17: Add lights and gauges to the brackets.

STEP 18: Gather the bricks shown for the wheels.

STEP 19: Build the wheel assembly as shown and attach it to the underside of the robot's body. The white plate goes in the front.

STEP 20: Gather the bricks shown. The third wheel attaches to the back of the robot and gives it a unique look.

STEP 21: Assemble the wheel as shown.

STEP 22: Attach the third wheel to the bracket on the back of the robot's body.

STEP 23: Gather the bricks shown—one set for each arm.

STEP 24: Assemble the arms as shown. Attach each arm to the body using the connector pin.

STEP 25: Add two 3 x 3 wedge plates to the body as well as a 2 x 2 turntable. Then attach the head.

Simon the Mechanical Robot is ready to roll! Set him up with scientists working on him and adding the last few parts or watch him zoom around as he helps build the robot lab!

SORVO THE SCUTTLE BOT
STEP-BY-STEP

This nimble little robot packs a lot of personality into a tiny body! His claw-like legs allow him to scuttle into tiny spots and even climb walls. What else can he do? Well, that's up to your imagination!

PARTS LIST

LIGHT GRAY BRICKS
1—2 x 4 wedge plate
2—1 x 1 plates with clip light (round hole)
2—1 x 1 plates with clip
2—1 x 2 plates with socket on the end
2—1 x 2 plates with one clip on top
1—2 x 2 round brick

DARK GRAY BRICKS
1—1 x 2 plate with handle on the side
2—1 x 2 plates with ball on the side
2—1 x 2 slopes, inverted

BLACK BRICKS
1—2 x 2 plate
1—2 x 2 plate, modified with octagonal bar frame
1—2 x 2 plate with turntable
2—antennas

ASSORTED BRICKS
2—1 x 1 translucent blue round plates
2—1 x 2 green curved slopes
4—barbs, large dark gray
4—arms mechanical, Bionicle/Exo-Force, ID 53989

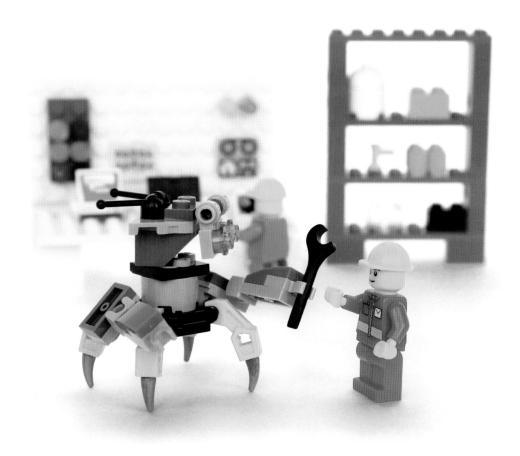

STEP 1: Gather the bricks shown.

STEP 2: Start with the black 2 x 2 plate. Add the octagonal brick, the light gray round brick and the 2 x 2 plate with turntable.

STEP 3: Add two 1 x 2 inverted slope bricks and the light gray 2 x 4 wedge plate.

STEP 4: Place the 1 x 2 plate with handle on the side and the antennas on top of the head. The eyes will attach to the ends of the handle.

STEP 5: Complete the head.

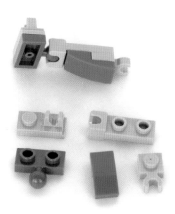

STEP 6: Assemble the arms as shown. The clip on the 1 x 2 light gray plate will attach the arm to the octagonal bar.

STEP 7: Assemble the legs as shown.

STEP 8: Complete the Scuttle Bot by attaching the arms and legs. Now he is ready to go skittering off on an adventure! Teach him how to use a wrench and he'll be quite helpful around the lab. Just be careful that he doesn't get into trouble—he's a tricky little guy!

SWERVE AND SLIDE: THE MINI ROBOTS

NO-INSTRUCTION CREATIVE CHALLENGE

Swerve and Slide are classic-looking robots. These simple robots can motor nimbly around the robot lab, helping with all kinds of tasks such as delivering tools to the workers. Adapt this design to create your own robots. Experiment with the types of arms, tools and eyes.

KEY ELEMENTS

Brackets for attaching eyes
1 x 2 plates, modified with handles and clips

1 x 2 grill
1 x 4 plate with hinges
Various basic bricks
Wheels

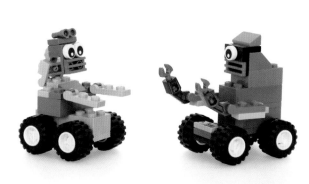

Start with a 2 x 6 plate and some wheels. Then build the body of the robot. Add arms with joints and bricks with gauges.

The top of this robot's head has a 1 x 2 plate with one stud on top and a pair of minifigure binoculars on top of that. The neck is posable.

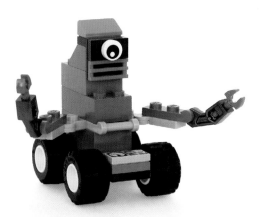

This robot's arms can move up and down at the elbow and can also move in and out from the shoulder.

Use 1 x 4 plates with hinges to make the shoulders move. The brick used in the forearm is LEGO ID 53989.

ROBOT WORKSPACE
NO-INSTRUCTION CREATIVE CHALLENGE

Scientists develop robots to perform repetitive tasks so that humans don't have to do them. Robots also perform tasks that might be dangerous for humans, such as working in outer space or at the bottom of the ocean. They are used in factories to build cars, electronics and other products. The lives of people are improved through the use of robotic limbs and other inventions. Use your LEGO bricks to build a robot lab for engineering robots and inventing new machines. What new invention will come to life in your robot lab?

KEY ELEMENTS

DESK

Translucent 1 x 1 round plates to use as lights
6 x 12 plate for the wall board
Slope bricks with computer screens
Tiles, decorated with gauges
Brackets to hold the wall board
Chair—ours is made higher with a 2 x 2 brick

SHELF

4—2 x 8 plates
18—1 x 2 bricks
Nozzle and 1 x 1 round brick for building a fire extinguisher
Round bricks and domed bricks to look like supplies

TOOL CART

1—4 x 6 dark gray plate
1—4 x 6 yellow plate
1—1 x 6 bar with four studs
8—small wheels
Steering wheel
Bricks and plates modified with clips for holding the tools
Various bricks for building the tool cart
Tools

This robot lab is equipped with a desk, computers and a shelf for supplies. These are the perfect places for workers to store their tools and materials.

This handy tool cart is perfect for moving supplies.

Use a 1 x 2 brick with a horizontal clip and a 1 x 2 plate with an arm up to attach the tool cart to the trailer. This allows the cart to pull the trailer and the trailer will also turn.

The desk and the board behind it are two separate elements. Use two brackets 1 x 2—2 x 2 to attach a 6 x 12 plate to the legs.

The workers need a step ladder in order to access the largest robot.

Just be careful that nothing goes wrong with the wiring! And be sure to build a fire extinguisher just in case.

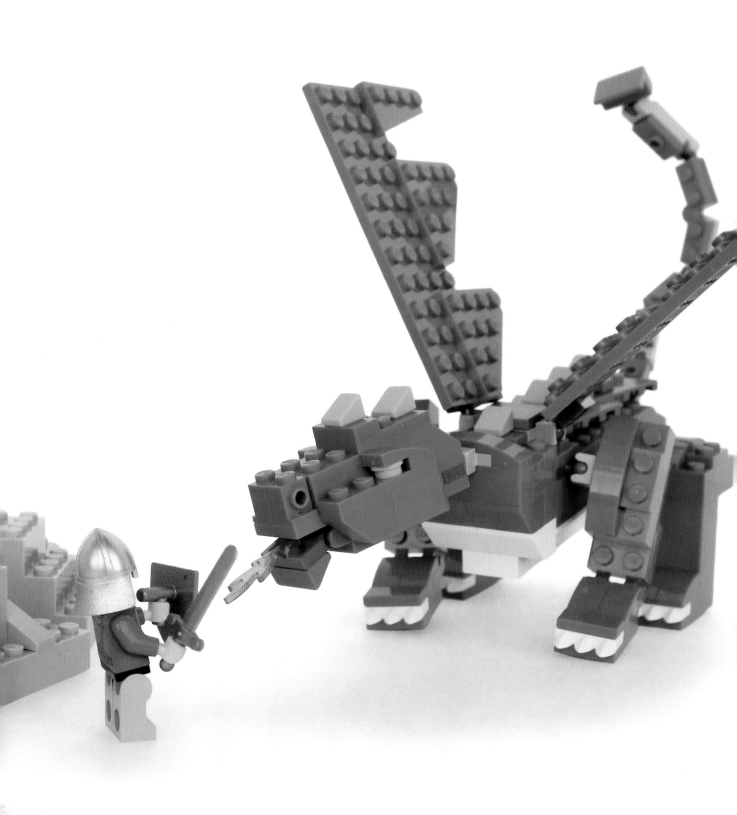

CHAPTER 2

THE WORLD OF KNIGHTS AND DRAGONS

Create your own fairy tale world in which knights protect the countryside and dragons make a terrifying appearance! Defeat the enemy with Medieval-inspired projects—a siege tower (page 45), a catapult (page 40) and a working crossbow (page 42). The most fun might be the dragons! These posable beasts with their mighty wings, sharp claws and fiery breath are perfect for epic battles straight from your imagination.

LEGENDARY FIRE-BREATHING DRAGON
STEP-BY-STEP

Almost every culture in the world has legends of encounters with dragons—fascinating flying beasts with the power to breathe fire. This classic dragon looks as though it is ready to jump from the pages of a storybook and into a duel with LEGO knights! Ball and socket joints make this dragon fully posable, allowing it to assume almost any position.

PARTS LIST
BODY

GREEN BRICKS

13—2 x 4 plates
8—2 x 2 plates
4—4 x 4 plates
3—2 x 3 plates
2—1 x 4 plates
1—2 x 6 plate
10—1 x 2 plates
6—1 x 2 plates, one stud on top
3—1 x 2 plates, modified with handle on the side
2—1 x 2 plates, modified with clips on the side
2—2 x 4 wedge plates, right
2—2 x 4 wedge plates, left
2—1 x 2 bricks
8—2 x 4 bricks
1—1 x 4 brick
6—2 x 2 bricks
2—1 x 1 bricks, modified with a stud on the side
2—2 x 3 bricks, curved end
1—1 x 2 slope, 30 degree
2—1 x 2 slopes
10—1 x 2 curved slopes
7—1 x 4 curved slopes, double, no studs
4—1 x 2 slopes, inverted
2—2 x 2 slopes, inverted
2—1 x 2 tiles

WHITE BRICKS

1—2 x 6 plate
2—2 x 4 plates
1—1 x 2 plate
4—2 x 2 slopes, inverted
4—2 x 4 slopes, double inverted
4—1 x 2 plates, modified with three claws

LIME GREEN BRICKS

2—1 x 1 round plates
1—2 x 2 plate
6—1 x 1 slopes, 30 degree

RED BRICKS

1—1 x 2 plate with clips on the side
1—fire

GRAY BRICKS

8—dark gray 1 x 2 plates, modified with ball on side
7—light gray 1 x 2 plates, modified with small ball socket on side

WINGS

GREEN BRICKS

2—4 x 12 plates
1—2 x 4 wedge plate, right
1—2 x 4 wedge plate, left
4—4 x 4 wedge plates, corner
1—2 x 2 tile

TAIL

GRAY BRICKS

1—1 x 2 plate, modified with handle on the end
1—1 x 2 plate modified with a handle on one end and a socket on the other
2—1 x 2 plates with clips
1—1 x 2 plate with socket on end
1—1 x 2 plate with a ball on one end and a socket on the other
1—1 x 2 plate, modified with ball on the side

GREEN BRICKS

2—1 x 2 plates with one stud on top
2—1 x 2—1 x 2 hinges
1—1 x 2 panel

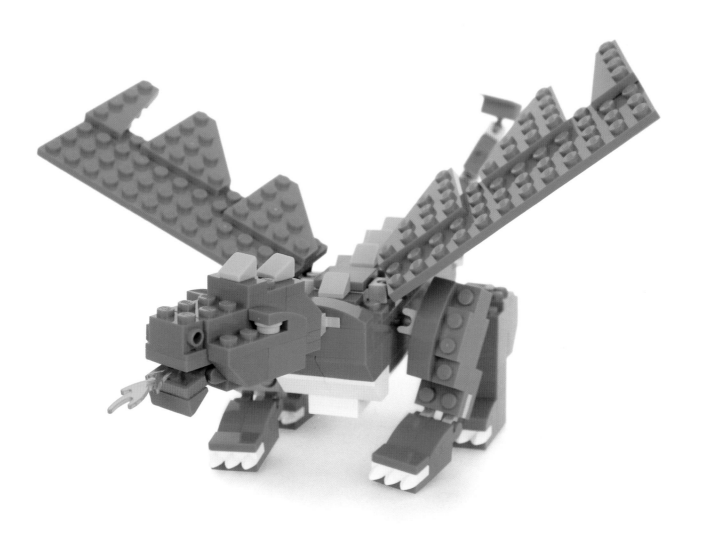

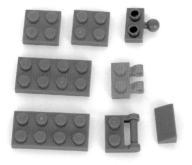

STEP 1: Gather these bricks for the dragon's mouth.

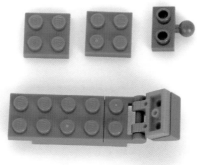

STEP 2: Assemble the dragon's jaw.

STEP 3: The picture shows two 2 x 2 plates, but it would also work to substitute a 2 x 4 green plate. The red plate will be the dragon's mouth.

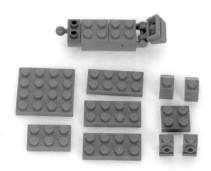

STEP 4: Gather these bricks for the dragon's head.

STEP 5: Line up a 2 x 3 green plate and a 2 x 4 green plate. On top of these, add two 1 x 1 bricks with a stud on the side, a 4 x 4 plate and two 1 x 2 green slope bricks.

STEP 6: Stack two 2 x 4 green plates and a 2 x 2 green plate. Add these to the head.

STEP 7: This is what the side of the head should look like at this point.

STEP 8: Add a 1 x 2 green brick, a 1 x 2 inverted slope, a lime green 1 x 1 round plate and a 1 x 2 green curved slope to each side of the face.

STEP 9: Build the spikes on the dragon's head. Place two 1 x 2 green plates with one stud on top on the top of the head, along with two 1 x 1 lime green slopes.

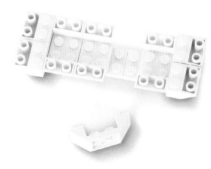

STEP 10: Build the dragon's body. Start with a white 2 x 6 plate, a white 2 x 4 plate and a white 1 x 2 plate on the head end of the body.

STEP 11: Add two white 2 x 2 inverted slopes. Each of these bricks covers one stud on the 1 x 2 white plate from step 10.

STEP 12: Add four white 2 x 4 double inverted slope bricks and two 2 x 2 white inverted slope bricks on the end. The double inverted slopes will create the dragon's belly.

STEP 13: Add a 2 x 4 white plate on the tail end of the dragon.

STEP 14: Place two 4 x 4 green plates on the middle of the body.

STEP 15: This layer has (from left to right) a 2 x 4 plate, two 1 x 2 dark gray plates with a ball on the side, four 2 x 4 green bricks and two green 2 x 2 inverted slopes.

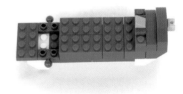

STEP 16: Gather the bricks shown.

STEP 17: On the head end of the dragon, add a 1 x 4 green brick and two 2 x 4 green plates stacked on top of each other.

STEP 18: Place a 1 x 2 light gray plate with a socket on the side at the head end of the dragon. Then add (from front to back) a 1 x 4 green curved slope on top of the socket and another 1 x 4 green curved slope. Then add a 1 x 4 green plate with a 1 x 2 green plate with one stud and a 1 x 1 lime green slope on top of it.

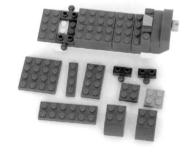

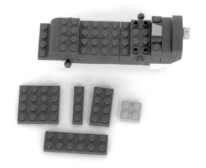

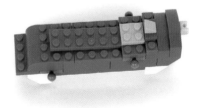

STEP 19: Find the bricks shown.

STEP 20: Add two 2 x 3 green bricks with curved ends to the tail end of the dragon. Build the sockets for the front legs by adding two 1 x 2 light gray plates with a ball on the side and a 2 x 2 green plate between them.

STEP 21: Fill in the back of the dragon with the 4 x 4 green plate and the 1 x 4 green plate. Then add a 2 x 4 green plate and a lime green 2 x 2 plate over the front leg sockets. Place the 2 x 6 green plate in the middle of the back.

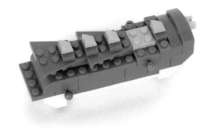

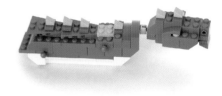

STEP 22: Build two spikes for the back as shown.

STEP 23: Then add them to the back of the dragon.

STEP 24: Attach the head to the body.

STEP 25: Gather the bricks shown for each back leg.

STEP 26: Start with a 2 x 4 green plate, a 1 x 2 white plate with claws and two 1 x 2 green plates stacked just behind the claws.

STEP 27: Cover the claws with two 1 x 2 green curved slopes and build the leg as shown.

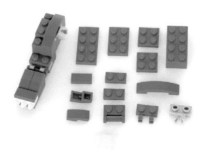

STEP 28: The completed hind legs should look like this.

STEP 29: Gather the bricks shown for the front legs. One set for each leg.

STEP 30: Start with a 2 x 3 green plate, a 1 x 2 white plate with claws and a 2 x 2 green plate.

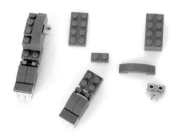

STEP 31: Add a 1 x 2 green tile (or substitute with a 1 x 2 green plate) and a 1 x 2 green plate with a handle on the side.

STEP 32: Add two 1 x 2 green curved slopes and a 1 x 2 green plate with clips on the side.

STEP 33: Place a 2 x 2 green plate under the 1 x 2 green plate with clips. Then add a 1 x 2 green plate.

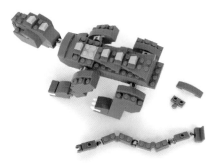

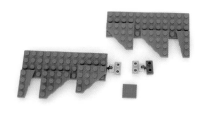

STEP 34: Attach a 2 x 4 green plate to the leg on top of the 1 x 2 green plate with clips. Then build the top of the leg as shown.

STEP 35: Build the tail and attach it to the body with a ball socket.

STEP 36: Assemble the wings as shown.

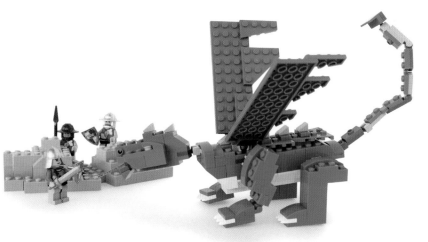

STEP 37: Attach the wings. The fire does not attach to the mouth—it is held in place by closing the mouth around the fire.

The knight is trying his best to be brave, but this fire-breathing dragon makes even the strongest knight's knees quiver! And look, his friends are hiding behind the rocks! Some help they are!

RED SERPENT DRAGON

STEP-BY-STEP

This dragon is inspired by the serpent-like dragons of Asia. He is fierce and yet mysterious, preferring to hide in caves out of the sight of humans. This nimble dragon seems to glide through the air with his leathery wings, swooping down every now and then to catch a fish from a stream.

PARTS LIST

RED BRICKS
2—4 x 4 plates
3—2 x 2 plates
4—1 x 2 plates
2—4 x 6 plates
1—1 x 4 plate
1—2 x 8 plate
1—2 x 6 plate
1—2 x 4 plate
2—1 x 6 plates
4—1 x 2 plates, one stud on top
2—1 x 1 plates, clip on the side
1—1 x 2 plate, clips on the side
1—1 x 2 plate, handle on the side
1—2 x 3 wedge plate, right
1—2 x 3 wedge plate, left
1—3 x 4 wedge plate with stud notches
2—1 x 1 round plates
2—2 x 8 bricks
5—1 x 2 bricks
10—2 x 2 bricks
2—2 x 4 bricks
2—1 x 3 bricks

4—1 x 2 slopes, inverted
2—1 x 2 slopes
2—2 x 2 slopes
4—1 x 2 slopes, 30 degree
8—1 x 1 slopes, 30 degree
2—1 x 2 slopes, 45 degree triple
2—1 x 3 curved slopes
4—2 x 2 x ⅔ high curved slopes
1—1 x 2 tile
2—helmet plumes

DARK RED BRICKS
1—2 x 4 plate
2—1 x 2 plates or 1—2 x 2 plate
2—1 x 4 plates
4—3 x 3 wedge plates, corner
2—4 x 4 wedge plates, corner
2—2 x 4 wedge plates, right
2—2 x 4 wedge plates, left
1—3 x 6 wedge plate, right
1—3 x 6 wedge plate, left

TAN BRICKS
2—2 x 4 plates
4—1 x 2 plates

4—1 x 2 plates, modified with 3 claws
3—2 x 2 slopes, inverted
1—2 x 6 brick
1—1 x 2 brick

BROWN BRICKS
2—2 x 3 plates
1—3 x 8 wedge plate, right
1—3 x 8 wedge plate, left

LIME GREEN BRICKS
2—1 x 1 round plates

WHITE BRICKS
1—1 x 2 plate, modified with 3 claws

GRAY BRICKS
4—1 x 2 dark gray plates, ball on the side
3—1 x 2 light gray plates, socket on the side
2—1 x 2 light gray plates, socket on the end
1—1 x 2 plate, handle on the end
1—1 x 2 plate, clip on the end

PURPLE
8—1 x 1 slopes, 30 degree

STEP 1: Gather these pieces for the dragon's head.

STEP 2: Stack two 4 x 4 red plates. Then add the green eyes, a 2 x 2 red plate and two 1 x 2 red plates.

STEP 3: Add two 1 x 3 red curved slope bricks and two 1 x 1 red slope bricks.

STEP 4: Place the two 2 x 3 red wedge plates on the head. They should cover one row of studs on the head and then hang off in the front. Add two 1 x 1 red round plates just behind those.

STEP 5: Add the 3 x 4 red wedge plate and the white teeth.

STEP 6: Turn the dragon's head over and gather the pieces shown for building the underside of the head.

STEP 7: Add two red 1 x 2 inverted slopes on each side of the head. Place a 2 x 2 red plate in the middle as well as a 1 x 2 dark gray plate with a ball on the side, a 1 x 2 red plate with a handle and a 1 x 2 red plate with clips. The two red plates allow the mouth to open and close.

STEP 8: Add a 2 x 4 dark red plate and two 1 x 2 dark red plates (or a 2 x 2) under the head.

STEP 9: Turn the head back over and add two 1 x 1 red plates with a clip on the side. These can each hold a triple feather plume or something similar.

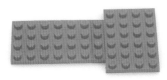

STEP 10: Line up the plates shown for the base of the dragon's body.

STEP 11: Add to the body—two 2 x 8 red bricks (or the equivalent), two 1 x 2 red slope bricks, two 2 x 2 red slope bricks, one 1 x 2 red brick and a dark gray 1 x 2 plate with a ball on the side. Stack the two 1 x 2 red plates and put the light gray 1 x 2 plate with socket on the top. Place this on the middle two studs in the front of the body.

STEP 12: Add a 2 x 8 red plate, a 2 x 2 red plate and two 1 x 2 dark gray plates with a ball on the side. These will be the wing sockets.

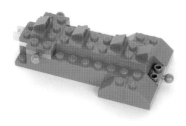

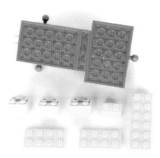

STEP 13: Add to the body—one 2 x 4 red plate, one 2 x 6 red plate, four 1 x 2 plates with one stud on top and four purple slopes.

STEP 14: Add slope bricks to the sides of the body. Place two 1 x 1 red slopes on the front of the body and one 1 x 2 red tile over the joint that will hold the tail.

STEP 15: Gather the tan bricks shown for the underside of the dragon's body.

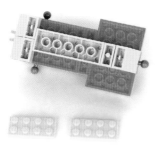

STEP 16: Build the underside of the dragon's body.

STEP 17: Add the two 2 x 4 tan plates and two 1 x 3 red bricks to the dragon's belly

STEP 18: Build the front and back legs. Each foot has a tan 1 x 2 plate with three claws and a tan 1 x 2 plate.

STEP 19: Assemble the tail. If you have more joint pieces, you can make the tail longer or give it more joints.

STEP 20: Attach the dragon's head and tail to the body.

STEP 21: Build the wings as shown. If you don't have these exact bricks, experiment with what you have!

STEP 22: This photo shows the underside of the wings.

STEP 23: Attach the wings and the dragon is complete.

Now it's time to play! Build your dragon a cave or a dragon's lair. Then send your knights on a quest through the forest. Will they meet up with the dragon?

The knights have stopped for a picnic lunch. The forest is calm and peaceful, or so it seems....

Little do they know that danger is lurking just on the other side of those rocks in a hidden cave!

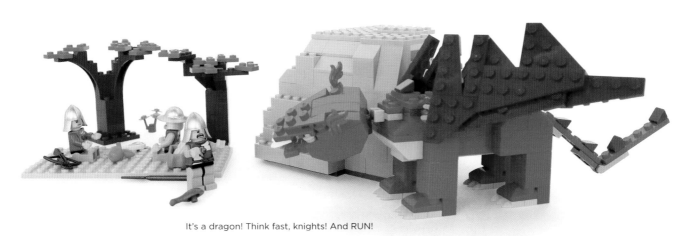

It's a dragon! Think fast, knights! And RUN!

FOREST AMBUSH CATAPULT

NO-INSTRUCTION CREATIVE CHALLENGE

Most LEGO catapults rely on a simple axle to create a lever, but this catapult harnesses the energy of a rubber band. The key to building a good LEGO catapult is to build it strong enough that it can withstand the force of the rubber band without breaking apart. This catapult shoots well on a minifigure scale! It's not going to shoot all the way across the room, but your minifigure knights will be pleased with its power. Try experimenting with the angle of your shooting arm to optimize your catapult's performance. Will a thicker rubber band cause the catapult to shoot farther? How about two rubber bands? Can you modify the design of the catapult so that it can withstand more torque from the rubber band?

PARTS LIST

(COLORS LISTED ARE AS PICTURED, BUT SPECIFIC COLORS ARE NOT IMPORTANT FOR THIS PROJECT!)

DARK GRAY BRICKS
1—4 x 4 plate
2—1 x 8 bricks
2—1 x 2 Technic bricks
4—1 x 2 Technic bricks with an X hole
2—1 x 6 Technic bricks

2—1 x 14 Technic bricks
2—Technic axles, 8 studs

LIGHT GRAY BRICKS
1—1 x 6 Technic brick
2—1 x 6 bricks
1—Technic axle, 8 studs
1—Technic axle, 3 studs

RED BRICKS
1—2 x 6 brick
1—1 x 6 brick

4—Technic bushes

ASSORTED BRICKS
4—1 x 2 light blue bricks
2—1 x 4 light blue bricks
1—1 x 13 white Technic liftarm
2—black connector pins
Various bricks to add stability to the frame, if needed

Rubber band

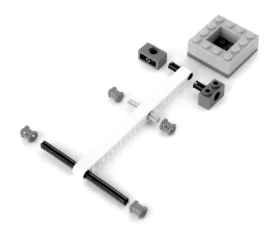

An effective catapult has a basket that is as close as possible to the same size as the object being launched. We found that it works well to shoot 2 x 2 round bricks from a 2 x 2 opening. Load the 2 x 2 round bricks on their sides into the basket.

Assemble the shooting arm as shown. The brick that we used for the shooting arm is a 1 x 13 Technic liftarm. Use black connector pins to attach 1 x 2 Technic bricks to the first two holes in the shooting arm. These bricks will hold the basket.

The little red pieces are called Technic bushes and they keep the axles from sliding out of the liftarm. The black pins make a tight connection and do not allow the Technic bricks to turn.

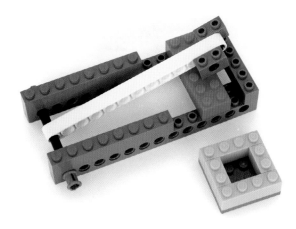

Build a frame for the catapult. Slide the Technic axle through one Technic brick, then through the shooting arm and then through the other Technic brick. Secure it with a Technic bush on each side. Then attach the basket to the shooting arm.

Finish building the frame. The axles that run across the top of the catapult stop the shooting arm and cause it to release the projectile at about a 45 degree angle. Attach the rubber band to the top axle with a loop knot. Then feed it under the lower axle and stretch it around the shooting arm. The small gray axle that sticks out on the shooting arm keeps the rubber band from sliding down the shooting arm, making the catapult more efficient.

Now it's time to play! See how far your catapult will shoot. Build two catapults and you can have a battle with a friend. Or see how well your knights can defend themselves against one of the dragons.

RAMPART CROSSBOW

STEP-BY-STEP

Rampart crossbows are large crossbows with bow spans around 13 feet that were secured to stands or carts. They were used in Europe in the 14th century. This LEGO crossbow launches 2 x 2 round bricks with impressive force. Your LEGO knights will appreciate having this powerful weapon in their arsenal as they battle dragons and more. It's the perfect addition to your knights and dragons world!

PARTS LIST

BROWN BRICKS
3—1 x 6 plates
1—1 x 10 plate
1—2 x 10 plate
2—1 x 1 round plates

2—1 x 12 bricks
5—2 x 2 slopes, inverted
2—1 x 4 tiles or plates

ASSORTED BRICKS
2—2 x 6 black plates
5—2 x 4 tan plates

3—2 x 4 light gray tiles (must be tile)
1—light gray bracket 2 x 2—1 x 1, inverted
1—large rubber band
2 x 2 round bricks for projectiles

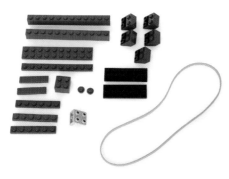

STEP 1: This photo contains everything needed to build the frame of the crossbow.

STEP 2: Start with two black 2 x 6 plates, a 2 x 10 brown plate and the inverted bracket.

STEP 3: Add four 2 x 2 inverted slope bricks to the front of the crossbow. Add two 1 x 12 bricks to the center of the crossbow, starting on the second stud behind the bracket.

STEP 4: Build the front of the crossbow as shown. Stretch the rubber band around the back of the crossbow. The bricks on the front may bend slightly under the pressure, but the crossbow will hold together.

STEP 5: Add the tan 2 x 4 plates and the gray tiles to the crossbow. The tiles create a smooth surface for the projectile to slide on. Without tiles, the projectile would catch on the studs of the bricks and would not fire with much force.

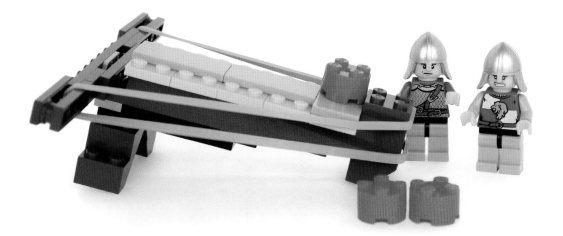

Stretch both ends of the rubber band around the back of the crossbow. Load the 2 x 2 round brick onto the crossbow.

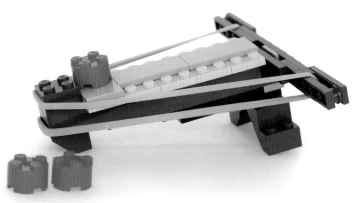

To shoot the crossbow, simply release the top loop of the rubber band. It will spring forward, launching the LEGO projectile!

SIEGE TOWER
NO-INSTRUCTION CREATIVE CHALLENGE

The siege tower was a large wooden tower on wheels used in the Roman Empire and also during the Middle Ages in Europe to protect attackers as they stormed a castle or fortress. If an army wished to conquer a castle, they were up against high walls, strong fortifications and soldiers shooting down at them from above. The siege tower, which could be as large as three stories high, offered protection from arrows and catapults while also allowing the attackers to breach the high castle walls. Since they were so large, siege towers were usually constructed at the site and used only as a last resort when other methods of attack had failed. Gather your LEGO knights with their crossbows and build them this protective siege tower! They will be ready for any battle!

KEY ELEMENTS

Various brown and tan bricks
Ladder with clips
1—4 x 8 brown plate

2—6 x 8 brown plates
1—1 x 6 brown plate
2—1 x 2 plates with a clip on the end
2—1 x 2 plates with a handle on the end

1—1 x 2 plate with a handle on the side (open ends)
1—6 x 8 gray plate and 1—4 x 6 gray plate for the base of the tower
4—wheels without tires

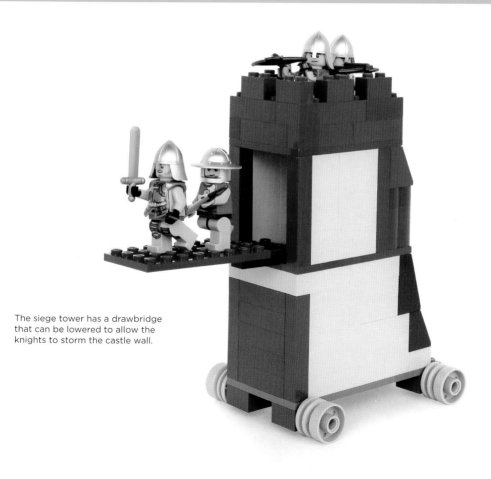

The siege tower has a drawbridge that can be lowered to allow the knights to storm the castle wall.

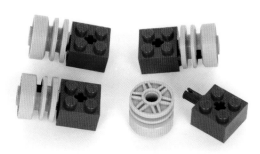

These are the wheels used for the tower.

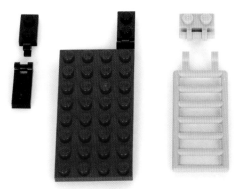

Use 1 x 2 plates modified with clips and handles to make a working drawbridge.

The drawbridge can be lowered when it's time for the attackers to run onto the castle wall.

Use 1 x 2 bricks to create openings around the top of the tower for the archers to shoot through.

The knights are safe behind the walls of the tower. They can shoot their crossbows through the openings at the top of the walls.

The knights can hide inside the tower as it is rolled toward the castle. Pushing a real siege tower was a huge undertaking! The tower might be full of the weight of about 200 soldiers and the ground was often full of ruts, bumps and mud.

CHAPTER 3

CARS, TRUCKS AND THINGS THAT FLY!

Cars, trucks and all kinds of space vehicles are probably the most popular things to build with LEGO bricks. Whether you're creating a truck, a race car or a space cruiser, it's fun to create a design and then change it again into something new. Build space flyers with wings that fold into different configurations. Assemble a massive fighter jet or create a Formula 1 race car complete with a pit crew and driver. It's always a fun day with LEGO vehicles!

...HTER JET
...-BY-STEP

Ru... the skies with this amazing fighter jet! This jet is styled after an F-22 Raptor, a single seat stealth tactical fighter that can reach speeds of over two times the speed of sound. This nimble aircraft can cruise at speeds above Mach 1 without the use of afterburners and it possesses cutting edge radar and sensor capabilities. Adapt the design to accommodate the wing pieces that you have on hand.

PARTS LIST

WHITE BRICKS
3—2 x 12 plates
2—6 x 12 wedge plates, right
2—6 x 12 wedge plates, left
1—6 x 2 wedge, right
1—6 x 2 wedge, left
1—2 x 2 slope, computer screen
2—3 x 6 white wedge bricks
2—tails 4 x 1 x 3

BLUE BRICKS
2—2 x 2 plates
1—1 x 2 plate
2—1 x 8 plates
3—2 x 3 plates
2—2 x 6 plates
1—2 x 8 plate
2—4 x 4 plates
1—2 x 4 plate
2—3 x 3 corner wedge plates
3—3 x 6 cut corners wedge plates
2—6 x 3 wedge plates, right

2—6 x 3 wedge plates, left
3—2 x 4 bricks
4—1 x 2 bricks
2—1 x 3 bricks
3—1 x 4 bricks
1—1 x 1 brick
2—2 x 2 bricks
1—1 x 6 brick
3—2 x 6 bricks
2—Technic axle pins with friction ridges, lengthwise

LIGHT GRAY BRICKS
1—6 x 6 plate
2—6 x 10 plates
2—3 x 6 wedge plates, right
2—3 x 6 wedge plates, left
3—2 x 2 plates with axle
5—2 x 4 bricks
1—1 x 4 brick
2—2 x 2 round bricks, with ridges
2—1 x 2 x 1⅓ bricks, modified with curved top
1—1 x 2 tile decorated with gauges

DARK GRAY BRICKS
1—bracket 1 x 2—2 x 2
1—3 x 8 wedge plate, right
1—3 x 8 wedge plate, left
1—2 x 2 curved slope
1—1 x 4 Technic brick

BLACK BRICKS
1—1 x 2 plate with clips
2—1 x 2 x 1⅓ bricks, modified with curved top
1—cockpit wind screen
1—2 x 2 cone
3—wheels
1—antenna

DARK RED BRICKS
2—3 x 12 wedge plates, right
2—3 x 12 wedge plates, left

NAVY BLUE BRICKS
1—3 x 8 wedge plate, right
1—3 x 8 wedge plate, left

STEP 1: Start building the cockpit with three 2 x 12 white plates. Place one on the bottom and attach two more to that one as shown above.

STEP 2: Build the nose of the plane as shown.

STEP 3: Add blue bricks to each side. Add a layer of blue plates on top of the bricks, but leave the front stud uncovered on each side. Then gather the bricks shown.

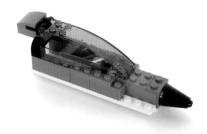

STEP 4: Add a computer screen to the cockpit. Place the antenna on top of a 1 x 1 brick. Add the two black curved bricks at the back of the cockpit.

STEP 5: Gather the pieces shown for building the wind screen.

STEP 6: Add a 2 x 3 blue plate on top of the black curved bricks. Add a 2 x 2 blue plate on top of that, followed by the 1 x 2 black plate with clips and the 2 x 2 light gray curved slope. Attach the wind screen to the clips.

STEP 7: Arrange a 6 x 6 light gray plate, a 2 x 3 blue plate and a 2 x 6 blue plate as shown.

STEP 8: Add a 6 x 10 light gray plate as shown.

STEP 9: Turn the body of the plane 180 degrees and add the plates shown.

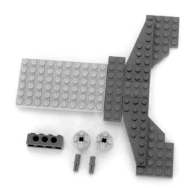

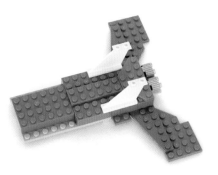

STEP 10: Build the horizontal stabilizers as shown. Find these bricks—two Technic blue axle pins with friction ridges (lengthwise), two 2 x 2 light gray round bricks with ridges and axle holes and a 1 x 4 dark gray Technic brick.

STEP 11: Build up the body of the plane as shown. Attach the round bricks to the Technic brick with the blue axle pins. Attach two 2 x 2 bricks to the underside of a 2 x 6 plate. Attach this to the body to fill in the hole that is shown.

STEP 12: Place the wedge plate on the back of the jet. Add two tail pieces to be the vertical stabilizers.

STEP 13: Add two 3 x 6 blue wedge plates and two 3 x 6 white wedge bricks.

STEP 14: Attach the cockpit to the body of the plane.

STEP 15: Build the wings as shown. Substitute similar wedge plate pieces as necessary.

STEP 16: Attach the wings to the body.

STEP 17: Find two light gray curved bricks. These will help hold the plane together.

STEP 18: Attach the curved bricks as shown.

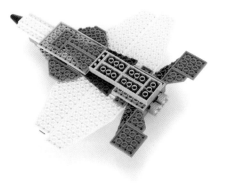

STEP 19: Turn the plane over on its back. This is how the underside should look so far.

STEP 20: Add more depth to the underside of the plane. Bricks shown are the following—two red 3 x 12 plates, five 2 x 4 light gray bricks, one 1 x 4 light gray brick, one 6 x 10 plate, two 3 x 6 blue wedge plates and one 2 x 4 blue plate.

STEP 21: Add wheels and the plane is complete!

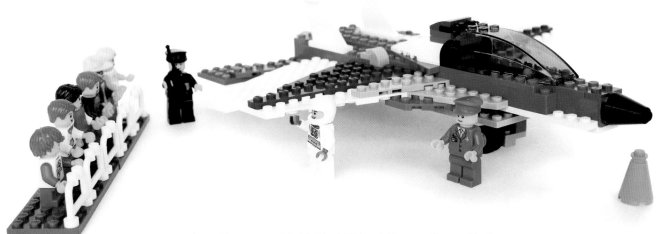

Put on an air show with your completed fighter jet! The minifigure audience will enjoy watching the pilot board the plane, take off and perform amazing loops and stunts! Add a security guard minifigure to keep the audience at a safe distance from the aircraft—this is a powerful machine!

FORMULA 1 RACE CAR

STEP-BY-STEP

Race to the finish with this Formula 1 style race car! Formula 1 cars are known for their open wheels, open cockpit and aerodynamic body design. They can accelerate to 60 miles per hour in less than 2 seconds! Build a pit crew too and you'll be ready for race day.

PARTS LIST

DARK GRAY BRICKS
1—12 x 4 vehicle base
2—1 x 2 plates
2—1 x 4 plates
1—3 x 6 wedge plate, right
1—3 x 6 wedge plate, left
1—2 x 6 slope, curved

LIME GREEN BRICKS
9—2 x 4 plates
2—2 x 6 plates
1—1 x 2 plate
2—1 x 1 round plates
2—1 x 1 slopes, 30 degree
4—1 x 2 slopes, curved
2—1 x 3 slopes, curved
2—1 x 2 slopes with four slots

2—2 x 3 wedge plates, right
2—2 x 3 wedge plates, left

ASSORTED BRICKS
2—2 x 4 plates with axles
1—steering wheel
2—front wheels
2—rear wheels (larger size)
1—seat

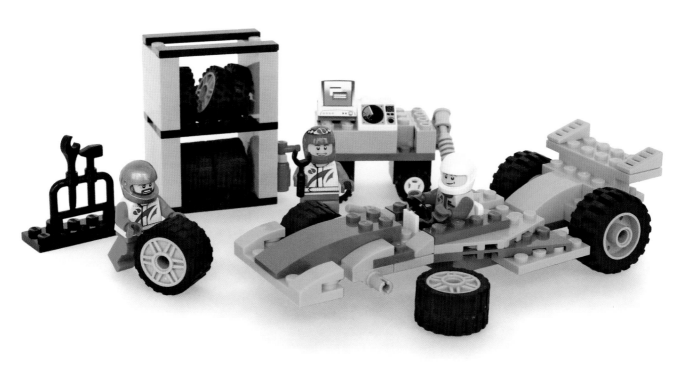

STEP 1: Find a 12 x 4 vehicle base and two 2 x 4 plates with axles. Formula 1 cars usually have back tires that are slightly larger than the front tires, so look for two sizes of wheels.

STEP 2: Attach the 2 x 4 plates with axles to the top of the vehicle base. This makes the car ride low to the ground. Then gather the pieces shown.

STEP 3: Add a 2 x 4 lime green plate, a 2 x 6 lime green plate and a dark gray 2 x 6 curved slope.

STEP 4: Add a 1 x 2 dark gray plate on each side of the gray curved slope. The front bumper has a 1 x 1 lime green round plate and a 1 x 2 lime green curved brick on each side.

STEP 5: Add the remaining bricks as shown. The lime green 1 x 2 plate is directly behind the gray curved slope.

STEP 6: Assemble the right and left sides of the car as shown.

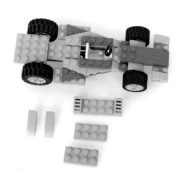

STEP 7: Add the sides to the car. Add a steering wheel and a seat.

STEP 8: Find the bricks shown.

STEP 9: Add three 2 x 4 lime green plates to the body of the car. Stack two 2 x 4 lime green plates on top of each other. Add the 1 x 2 lime green slopes with slots to the 2 x 6 plate.

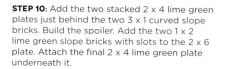

STEP 10: Add the two stacked 2 x 4 lime green plates just behind the two 3 x 1 curved slope bricks. Build the spoiler. Add the two 1 x 2 lime green slope bricks with slots to the 2 x 6 plate. Attach the final 2 x 4 lime green plate underneath it.

STEP 11: Place the spoiler on the back and you're ready for the race.

Look through your bricks—use tools and other elements to create a pit crew area. The tire rack shown is built out of 1 x 6 black plates and light gray bricks. Some computer screens and a flexible tube make a great air compressor for filling up tires.

The driver has his helmet on and he's ready to race!

DRAGSTER
NO-INSTRUCTION CREATIVE CHALLENGE

Drag racing is an exciting sport where racers compete two at a time on a short, straight racetrack. Many different types of vehicles are used in drag racing, but dragsters are known for their super long length and open wheel design. This awesome dragster is lightning fast and sure to come in first place!

KEY ELEMENTS

1—2 x 12 dark gray plate
1—2 x 8 dark gray plate
1—2 x 4 dark gray plate
1—2 x 6 light gray plate
3—2 x 4 light gray tiles

1—2 x 3 black wedge plate, right
1—2 x 3 black wedge plate, left
1—1 x 4 plate with angled tubes
2—rocker plates with rocker bearings
1—2 x 2 black curved slope
1—2 x 2 engine

1—steering wheel
2—small wheels
2—large wheels
1—seat
Various bricks for decoration—1 x 2 grills,
1 x 2 slope grills, etc.

The crowd goes wild as he approaches the finish line!

See if you can build a dragster using these photos as a guide.

The back of the car has a moveable fin and exhaust pipes.

Build the aerodynamic sides of the body with the pieces shown. The hinge brick is a rocker plate with rocker bearing. Build one of these for each side of the car.

The grill bricks are added to the wedge plate as shown.

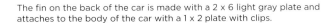

The fin on the back of the car is made with a 2 x 6 light gray plate and attaches to the body of the car with a 1 x 2 plate with clips.

The brick used for the exhaust pipes is a 1 x 4 plate, modified with angled tubes.

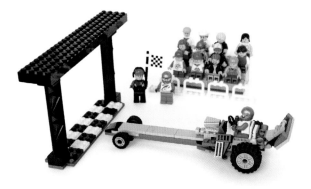

Build a race track for your dragster! Create a finish line with black and white 2 x 2 plates.

Create some stands for your minifigure audience to sit on by building a simple staircase with basic bricks.

MONSTER TRUCK
STEP-BY-STEP

Monster trucks got their start in the 1970s when people began equipping pickup trucks with gigantic wheels and suspension in order to compete with each other in mud bogging and truck pulling events. Today's monster trucks are more like giant dune buggies than pickup trucks and they compete in all kinds of events designed to showcase their skills. This big wheeled LEGO monster truck is ready for action, but can be built out of basic bricks rather than specific vehicle parts. Use the largest wheels that you have. If you have only smaller wheels, try adapting this design to create a smaller truck. Try building some ramps for your monster truck to jump off of or set up Hot Wheels cars for your truck to drive over.

PARTS LIST

DARK GRAY BRICKS
1—4 x 8 plate
2—4 x 6 plates
5—2 x 6 plates
5—1 x 6 plates
2—6 x 6 plates

LIGHT GRAY BRICKS
4—2 x 4 bricks
4—1 x 1 bricks, modified with a stud on one side
1—1 x 4 brick
2—2 x 4 plates, modified with axles

BLUE BRICKS
3—1 x 4 plates
2—1 x 6 plates
1—2 x 2 plate
1—4 x 4 plate
5—2 x 4 bricks
4—1 x 2 bricks
2—1 x 4 bricks
2—1 x 8 bricks
2—2 x 6 bricks
1—1 x 6 brick
4—1 x 1 bricks
8—2 x 1 slopes, inverted
2—1 x 1 slopes, 30 degree

5—1 x 4 tiles
2—doors

ASSORTED BRICKS
2—plates, modified 1 x 2 with ladder
2—1 x 6 bars with open studs
2—1 x 1 round translucent red plates
2—1 x 1 translucent yellow plates
1—3 x 6 windshield
1—steering wheel
4—wheels

STEP 1: Lay out a 4 x 8 dark gray plate, a 4 x 6 dark gray plate and two 2 x 6 dark gray plates as shown. This will form the base of the truck.

STEP 2: Add a 1 x 6 dark gray plate on each end.

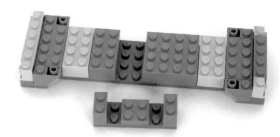

STEP 3: Build the spots for the headlights and tail lights. Front—two 1 x 1 light gray bricks with a stud on the front, one 1 x 4 light gray brick. Back—two 1 x 1 light gray bricks with a stud on the front, one 1 x 4 blue brick.

STEP 4: Add the bricks shown. The inverted slope bricks will create a space for the wheels. The 2 x 6 gray plate off to the side will provide a place for the driver to sit.

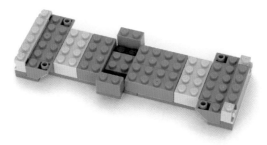

STEP 5: Put the seat in place.

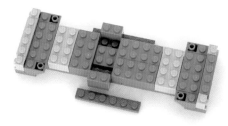

STEP 6: Add a 1 x 6 dark gray plate under the seat piece on both sides. One stud should show on the front end of the truck.

STEP 7: On each gray plate, add two 1 x 2 blue inverted slopes and one 1 x 2 blue brick.

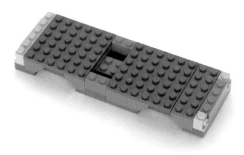

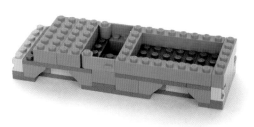

STEP 8: Cover the truck with gray plates, except for the seat.

STEP 9: Add doors to the cab. Add two 2 x 6 bricks to the front of the truck as shown and build the bed of the truck with blue bricks on the back.

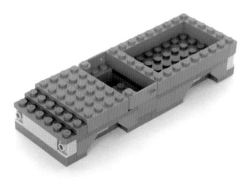

STEP 10: Add a gray 2 x 6 dark gray plate and a 1 x 6 dark gray plate to the front of the truck as shown.

  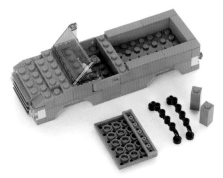

STEP 11: Add two 2 x 1 ladder bricks to create the grill on the front of the truck. Add a 1 x 6 blue plate directly behind that.

STEP 12: Add to the front of the truck one 4 x 4 blue plate and three 1 x 4 blue plates. There are two 1 x 4 blue plates on each side (starting on top of the stud on each door) and one on top of the ladders. Add two 1 x 1 blue slope bricks—one above each headlight. Gather the bricks shown to the right of the truck.

STEP 13: Add the windshield and the headlights and taillights. If you don't have tiles for the bed of the truck, just use regular plate bricks.

STEP 14: Add a 4 x 6 dark gray plate for the roof. You will need a 1 x 6 plate attached to the underside of the roof in order for it to sit flat (shown in Step 13). Add some wheels and some rails to the top of the truck and the truck is complete!

Now it's time for a monster truck rally! Build some small cars for your monster truck to crush as he rolls over them. Use basic bricks to create simple stands for the audience.

Then build a ramp for a ramp jumping contest! The audience is watching in excitement!

RUGGED PICKUP TRUCK

NO-INSTRUCTION CREATIVE CHALLENGE

This classic style pickup truck is ready to haul some cargo or head off on an adventure. With its powerful engine, there is no obstacle it can't get through! When you arrive at your destination, open the tailgate and grab your gear. Camping and fishing trips are even more fun when you have an awesome truck to take you there.

KEY ELEMENTS

1 x 4 hinge plates with swivel top for the opening doors

1 x 1 plates with clips and 1 x 2 plates, modified with a handle on the side (free ends) for building rear view mirrors

1 x 2 plate, modified with handle on the side, 1 x 2 plate, modified with clips on the side for building the working tailgate

Brackets, 1 x 2—1 x 2 inverted to hold the headlights and fog lights

1—1 x 2 hinge brick, for creating an opening hood

1 x 1 round bricks for exhaust pipes

2 x 1 slopes, inverted for building the wheel wells

Technic connectors and 1 x 1 round plates for building the engine components

1—2 x 6 windshield

1—2 x 4 windshield, no slope

Various gray plates and bricks for the body of the truck

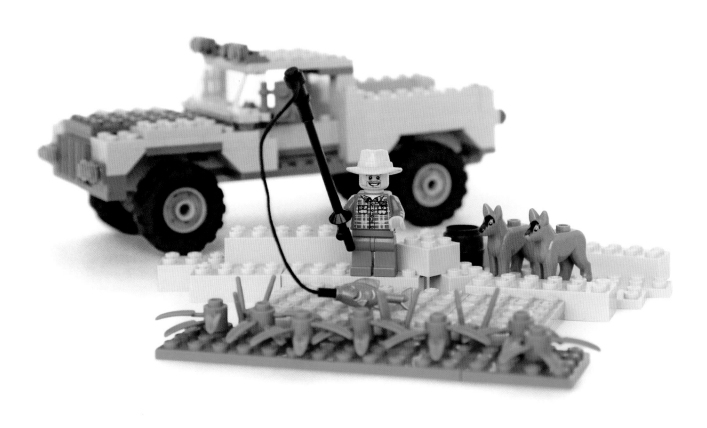

Attach the exhaust pipes (1 x 1 round plates and 1 x 1 round bricks) to a 1 x 4 brick with four studs on the side.

The tailgate attaches to the 1 x 4 brick as shown. Then the 1 x 4 brick attaches to the underside of the truck.

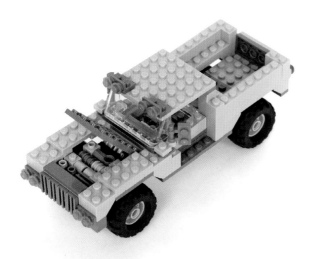

The hood opens with the help of a 1 x 2 hinge brick. Create an engine by using 1 x 1 round plates (stacked) and Technic connector bricks.

The tailgate opens with the help of plates with handles and clips.

When your truck is complete, load it up with camping, hunting or fishing gear and send your minifigures off on an adventure! The dogs love to ride in the back of the truck.

Make the doors open and close with 1 x 4 hinge plates with a swivel top or just use LEGO car doors if you have them.

The dogs love riding the in truck and feeling the breeze in their fur.

MOTORCYCLE
STEP-BY-STEP

A classic motorcycle is the perfect vehicle for your minifigures to cruise around LEGO town! Since a minifigure can't straddle a motorcycle seat, they have to ride either sitting or standing up. Convert this motorcycle to one that a minifigure can ride standing up by removing the three 2 x 2 plates and replacing them with a 1 x 2 brick and an open space. Either way, it's sure to be the fastest motorcycle in town!

PARTS LIST

BLUE BRICKS
2—1 x 2 plates, handle on the side
1—1 x 2 plate, one stud on top
3—2 x 2 plates
2—2 x 2 slopes, inverted
4—1 x 1 slopes, 30 degree
2—1 x 3 curved slopes

DARK GRAY BRICKS
2—2 x 3 plates
2—2 x 2 plates
2—1 x 2 plates
1—1 x 2 plate, one stud on top
2—1 x 2 Technic bricks with axle hole
1—1 x 2 brick
1—1 x 2 tile
1—bracket 1 x 2—1 x 2, inverted
1—1 x 1 plate, clip on top

LIGHT GRAY BRICKS
4—Technic axles, 3 studs long

BLACK BRICKS
1—2 x 6 plate
2—1 x 2 Technic bricks with axle holes
1—bracket 1 x 2—1 x 2, inverted
4—Technic liftarms 1 x 4, thin
1—handle bar
2—wheels

STEP 1: Gather the bricks shown.

STEP 2: Start with the 2 x 6 black plate on the bottom. Add the 1 x 2 Technic bricks and the 1 x 2 blue plates.

STEP 3: Insert two of the gray axles as shown.

STEP 4: Use the Technic liftarms and two more gray axles to attach the wheels to the motorcycle body.

STEP 5: Add a 2 x 2 blue inverted slope and a 2 x 3 plate to the front of the motorcycle. Directly behind the slope brick, add two 1 x 2 light gray plates and a 1 x 2 blue plate with one stud.

STEP 6: Gather the bricks shown.

STEP 7: Add a dark gray bracket to the front of the motorcycle and two 2 x 2 dark gray plates directly behind that. Add the handlebars.

STEP 8: Add four 1 x 1 blue slopes to the front of the motorcycle. Add the headlight.

STEP 9: Build the seat with a 2 x 2 blue plate and two 2 x 2 dark gray plates. Add a 2 x 2 blue inverted slope and a 1 x 2 dark gray brick to the back of the motorcycle. Then gather the pieces shown to the side of the motorcycle.

STEP 10: Add the taillights and the two 1 x 3 blue curved slopes to finish the motorcycle.

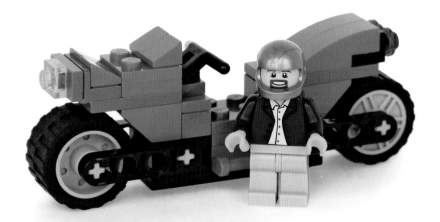

Find your minifigure a helmet and he'll be ready to roll!

Now it's time for your LEGO minifigure to go cruising around town or meet up with friends!

MINI JETS
STEP-BY-STEP

With a few basic bricks, you can build a pocket-sized jet that is ready for takeoff! Modify the wings and tail depending on which bricks you have on hand. These classic style jets are fun to zoom and they also look great displayed on a shelf.

PARTS LIST

DARK GRAY BRICKS
1—2 x 10 plate
1—2 x 3 plate
2—1 x 4 plates
3—2 x 2 plates
1—2 x 6 plate
1—1 x 2 plate
1—3 x 6 wedge plate, right

1—3 x 6 wedge plate, left
1—2 x 4 brick
1—2 x 2 brick
2—1 x 2 slopes, 30 degree
1—2 x 2 slope, inverted
1—bracket 2 x 1—2 x 2
1—1 x 2 grill

ORANGE BRICKS
1—2 x 2 cone

1—2 x 3 plate
1—1 x 2 plate
1—1 x 2 plate, one stud
1—1 x 4 tile

ASSORTED BRICKS
1—2 x 2 light gray slope
1—2 x 2 clear slope
1—2 x 2 light gray plate with axles
2—small wheels

STEP 1: Find the bricks shown.

STEP 2: Assemble the nose of the jet as shown.

STEP 3: Add a 2 x 4 dark gray brick, a 2 x 2 dark gray brick and a 2 x 2 dark gray inverted slope to the underside of the plane.

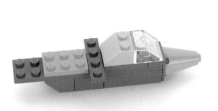

STEP 4: Add a 1 x 4 dark gray plate and a 2 x 3 orange plate as shown.

STEP 5: Add the wings and a 2 x 2 dark gray plate in between.

STEP 6: Place a 1 x 4 gray plate and a 1 x 4 orange tile (can also be a plate) across the wings. This helps to secure the wings. Add a 1 x 2 orange plate, a 2 x 2 dark gray plate and a 1 x 2 dark gray grill behind the wings. Then build the tail of the plane.

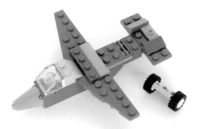

STEP 7: Add the 2 x 2 dark gray plate to the back of the plane and then add the tail and the last 1 x 2 plate.

STEP 8: Complete the jet by adding wheels. Now it's ready for takeoff! Try some loops and barrel rolls! Or build an airport with an air traffic control tower.

FOLDABLE FLYERS

STEP-BY-STEP

These pocket-sized mini flyers are constructed with joints that allow the wings to be posed in all different ways. They are fun to build and then fun to modify for a whole new look and their size makes them perfect for carrying around. LEGO fun on the go!

PARTS LIST

BLUE BRICKS
1—dark blue 4 x 6 plate
1—2 x 6 plate
1—2 x 2 plate
1—1 x 2 plate
2—flags 2 x 2 trapezoid
1—3 x 4 wedge plate with stud notches

BLACK BRICKS
1—2 x 2 plate
2—1 x 2 plates
1—bracket 2 x 2–1 x 2

1—translucent black slope curved 2 x 2 lip, no studs

LIME GREEN BRICKS
2—1 x 1 slopes, 30 degree
2—2 x 4 plates

GREEN BRICKS
2—1 x 2 plates, modified with handle on side

RED BRICKS
1—2 x 2 plate
1—1 x 2 plate
2—1 x 3 slopes

2—1 x 3 curved slopes
2—1 x 2 plates, modified with handle on side
1—slope curved 2 x 2 lip, no studs
8—1 x 1 translucent red round plates

GRAY BRICKS
1—dark gray 2 x 2 plate
1—dark gray tile, modified 2 x 2, inverted
2—dark gray slopes, 45 degree, 2 x 1 with ⅔ cutout
2—light gray 1 x 2 plates, modified with clips on side
2—antennas

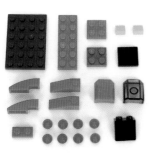

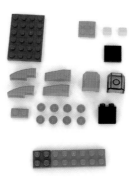

STEP 1: Gather the bricks shown. Color is not really important with this project. Be creative!

STEP 2: Line up a 2 x 2 gray plate and a 2 x 6 blue plate for the bottom of the flyer.

STEP 3: Add a 4 x 6 dark blue plate.

STEP 4: Place a 2 x 2 black plate, a 2 x 2 red plate and two 1 x 3 red slopes on top of the dark blue plate.

STEP 5: The two pieces added in this step are called slope curved 2 x 2 lip, no studs. The LEGO design ID is 30602.

STEP 6: Place the red 1 x 2 plate right behind the cockpit. Add the black bracket and the translucent red round bricks.

STEP 7: Add two 1 x 3 red curved slopes and the body of the flyer is finished.

STEP 8: Build the wings as shown.

STEP 9: Turn the flyer upside down and add a 1 x 2 dark gray slope with cutout, a 1 x 2 light gray plate with clips and a 1 x 2 black plate to each side.

STEP 10: Gather the bricks shown.

STEP 11: Add these bricks to the bottom of the plane.

STEP 12: Add the 2 x 2 inverted tile. This gives the plane a smooth underside for easy landings.

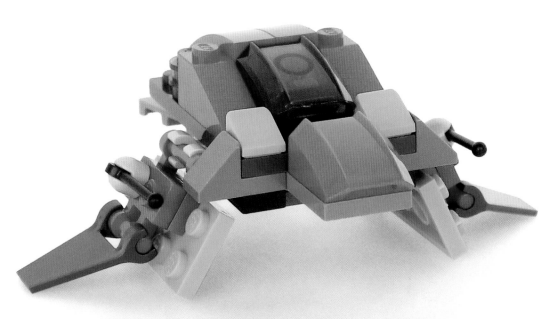

Fold the wings downward like this.

Or fold the wings upward like this and your flyer can glide through tight spaces.

Using the photos as a guide, see if you can build this second style of flyer.

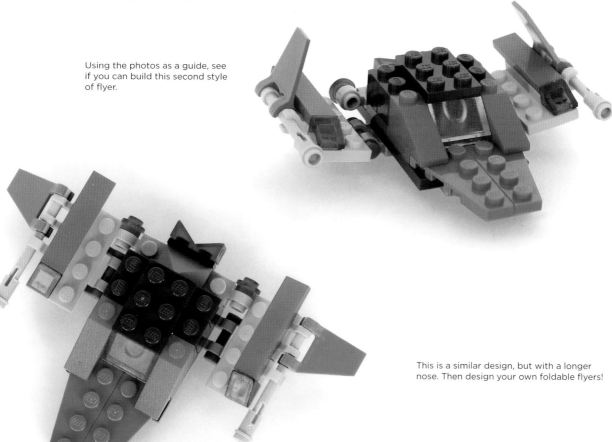

This is a similar design, but with a longer nose. Then design your own foldable flyers!

CLASSIC SPORTS CAR
STEP-BY-STEP

This Porsche-inspired sports car is ready to cruise around town! It's a classic-looking car and simple to build with basic bricks. After you build the car, try building some traffic lights. Create a drive-thru for your car to visit by making a building with a window on the side.

PARTS LIST

RED BRICKS
1—4 x 12 red plate
2—1 x 3 bricks
6—2 x 4 bricks
2—1 x 1 bricks
1—1 x 2 brick

1—1 x 4 brick, modified with four studs on the side
4—1 x 4 slopes
1—bracket 1 x 2—1 x 4
2—translucent 1 x 1 round plates

GRAY BRICKS
2—2 x 4 bricks with axles
1—1 x 4 brick

1—1 x 2 grill
2—1 x 1 round tiles

ASSORTED BRICKS
3—2 x 2 clear slopes
3—1 x 2 dark red grills
2—1 x 1 translucent yellow round plates
4—wheels

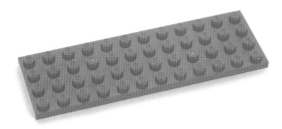

STEP 1: Start with a 4 x 12 plate. Use another color if you don't have red.

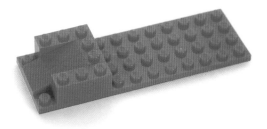

STEP 2: Add two 1 x 3 red bricks and two 1 x 4 red slopes.

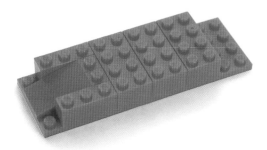

STEP 3: Add three 2 x 4 red bricks.

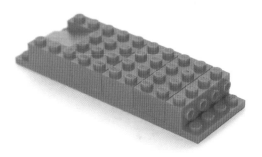

STEP 4: Add the 1 x 4 red brick with four studs on the side. The studs should face the back of the car.

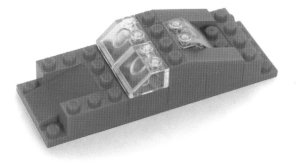

STEP 5: In this step, add three 2 x 2 clear slopes, one 1 x 2 red brick and two 1 x 4 red slopes.

STEP 6: Add the dark red grill pieces to the back of the car as shown. Gather the bricks shown for the bottom of the car.

STEP 7: Turn the car upside down and add three 2 x 4 red bricks, two dark gray bricks with axles, a 1 x 4 brick and the red bracket.

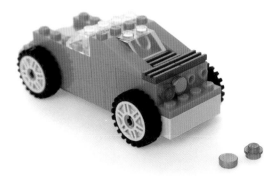

STEP 8: Add round gray tiles and translucent red bricks for the taillights.

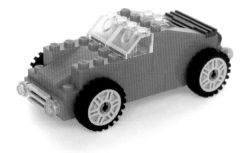

STEP 9: Finish the car by adding two 1 x 1 red bricks just behind the red bracket. Add the 1 x 2 grill and the two yellow translucent 1 x 1 round plates as headlights. Now your car is ready to cruise around town!

MINI VEHICLES
NO-INSTRUCTION CREATIVE CHALLENGE

These mini vehicles are easy to build and fun to play with. When you're building on a smaller scale, clear slope bricks work well for windshields and windows. Clear 1 x 2 bricks are also helpful for windows. What will you do with your mini vehicles? Try building a mini town to go with them by creating some simple buildings and roads.

PARTS LIST

FOR THE RED MINI SPORT UTILITY VEHICLE

RED BRICKS

1—2 x 6 brick
2—2 x 4 bricks
2—1 x 4 bricks modified with 4 studs on the side

2—1 x 1 bricks modified with a stud on the side
1—4 x 4 plate

ASSORTED BRICKS

2—2 x 2 plates with axles (black or dark gray)
1—1 x 2 dark gray ladder

4—2 x 2 clear slopes
2—1 x 1 translucent yellow round plates
1—1 x 2 dark gray grill
4—wheels

Build a little red SUV for off-road adventures!

STEP 1: Attach the wheels to a 2 x 6 brick.

STEP 2: Attach a 1 x 4 brick with 4 studs on the side on both the front and the back. Add the grill, headlights and taillights. Add two 2 x 4 bricks.

STEP 3: Add the four 2 x 2 clear slope bricks. The two on the sides should have the sloping side facing the center. Place two 1 x 1 bricks with a stud on the side on the back. Add the 4 x 4 plate for the roof and the ladder and the truck is finished.

Use the photos as a guide to build a tractor like this one or try your own design! The grill on the front of the tractor is made with a 1 x 2—2 x 2 bracket and two 1 x 2 grill bricks. To make it look like a tractor, you'll want to have larger wheels on the back than on the front.

The rear windshield is made from two clear 1 x 2 bricks.

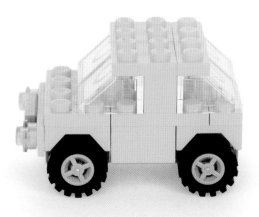

Here is another vehicle to try. This mini yellow car is cute, sporty and fast! The wheels have mudguards around them. They are 2 x 4 mudguards with two studs on each arch.

Use two 2 x 2 clear slopes for each windshield. The front grill and headlights are attached to a 1 x 2—1 x 4 bracket.

CHAPTER 4

IT'S A GREAT DAY IN LEGO TOWN

A LEGO town is the perfect project for a rainy day or any day! Find a large surface to work on and create houses, stores, a school or a library. In this chapter, you'll find a few ideas for some exciting elements to add to your LEGO town—a family amusement center, a vet's office, a playground and more. What will you add to your LEGO town? So many possibilities!

SKATE PARK
NO-INSTRUCTION CREATIVE CHALLENGE

Build a LEGO skate park! Minifigures can skate in style with their own half pipe and grinding rails. Be sure to build a park bench for spectators. After all, it's a lot more fun to perform awesome tricks when you have an audience!

KEY ELEMENTS

About 30 light gray slope bricks, some 2 x 2 and some 2 x 4

5—2 x 4 light gray tiles

1—1 x 4 gray tile

3—1 x 8 dark gray tiles

Light gray bricks

Light gray and dark gray plates for the bottom of each park element.

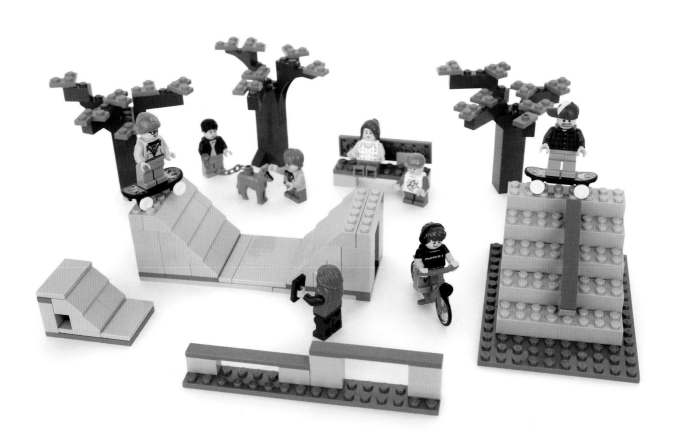

STEPS WITH GRINDING RAIL

Build a staircase with 2 x 4 bricks. A 1 x 8 tile works well for a grinding rail since its smooth surface allows the minifigure skateboards to slide. The grinding rail has 1 x 1 bricks to support it on each end and these are not attached to the stairs. The grinding rail is just resting in that position.

It's kind of scary up there at the top of the steps! It's a good thing this skater knows what he's doing.

Riding down on a bike is another thing, though. Yikes!

HALF-PIPE

No skate park would be complete without this classic feature! Sloped roof tile bricks are the key to an awesome half-pipe and the bottom of the half-pipe is covered with three 2 x 4 tiles and a 1 x 4 tile. If the top edges of your half-pipe are at least two studs wide, it's much easier to balance minifigures on skate boards on the top.

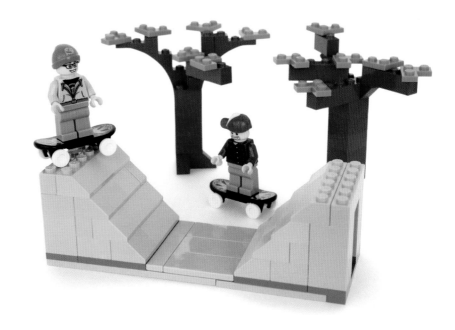

GRINDING RAIL AND SMALL JUMP

These two features are perfect to build if you don't have a lot of slope bricks. The grinding rail is the same concept at the one on the stairs. The small jump is built on a 4 x 6 gray plate.

GO-CART FAMILY ENTERTAINMENT CENTER

NO-INSTRUCTION CREATIVE CHALLENGE

Everyone will have fun at the LEGO family entertainment center! Build this exciting attraction with go-carts, video games, a concession stand and more. Then see if you can think of other games and features to add. A LEGO mini golf course would be fun to create!

PARTS LIST
GO CARTS

DARK GRAY BRICKS
1—2 x 4 plate
2—1 x 4 plates
1—2 x 6 plate
1—2 x 2 plate

RED BRICKS
1—2 x 2 brick
1—2 x 3 slope
2—1 x 1 slopes, 30 degree

ASSORTED BRICKS
1—1 x 2 white plate
1—2 x 4 white plate
2—2 x 2 black plates with axles
2—1 x 3 blue bricks
1—steering wheel
4—small wheels
Various gray bricks for building the race track

VIDEO GAMES

BLUE OR RED BRICKS
1—4 x 6 plate

2—1 x 4 plates
1—4 x 4 plate
8—1 x 4 bricks
2—2 x 6 bricks
1—1 x 3 brick
1—1 x 1 brick with a stud on the side
1—2 x 4 slope

ASSORTED BRICKS
3—1 x 4 or 2 x 4 black bricks for the video game screen
1 x 1 round plates in various colors for the video game controls

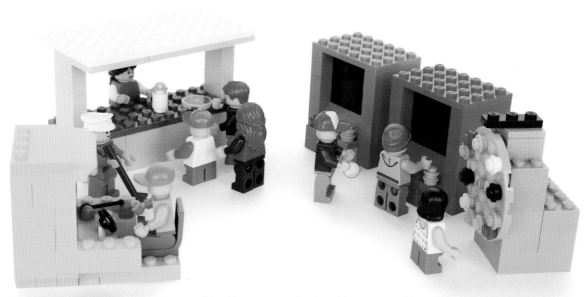

The video game area has two video game machines and a race car driving game. Guests can also try their luck at the spin-the-wheel game. Then they can head to the concession stand for a slice of pizza or a snack.

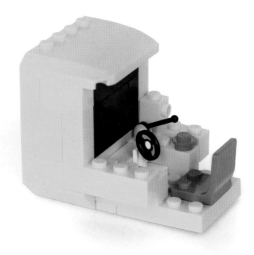

Each video game machine has two 2 x 6 bricks on the bottom and then a 4 x 4 plate. The 4 x 4 plate sticks out by one stud. Attach a 1 x 3 brick and a 1 x 1 brick with a stud on the side underneath the 4 x 4 plate. Then add a 2 x 4 slope, the black bricks for the screen and four 1 x 4 bricks on each side. Finish off the game with a 1 x 4 plate on each side and a 4 x 6 plate on the top. Use 1 x 1 round plates for the video game controls. Note that the back of the video game machine is open.

Try building a race car driving game with a seat and a steering wheel!

This spin-the-wheel game is simple to construct. Attach a round plate with a hole in the middle to a 2 x 2 brick with an axle. The wheel should spin freely. Use 1 x 1 round plates to decorate the wheel.

Which color will your minifigure need to land on to get the biggest prize?

So nice to see family members having such a good time together! This is what days off are all about.

Well, until one of them spills his drink! Good thing there was a janitor nearby.

After attempting the video games, it's time to head out to the go-carts!
Use gray bricks to build a boundary for the racetrack.

Build several go-carts in different colors.

Gather these pieces for building each go-cart.

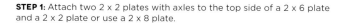

STEP 1: Attach two 2 x 2 plates with axles to the top side of a 2 x 6 plate and a 2 x 2 plate or use a 2 x 8 plate.

STEP 2: Add two 1 x 4 plates and a 2 x 4 plate to the body of the car as shown.

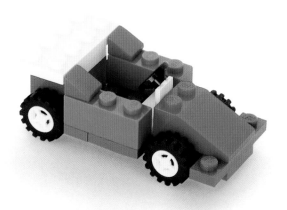

STEP 3: Add a 2 x 3 slope, two 1 x 3 bricks, a 2 x 2 brick and a 1 x 2 plate.

STEP 4: Complete the go-cart with a 2 x 4 plate and two 1 x 1 slopes.

VET'S OFFICE
NO-INSTRUCTION CREATIVE CHALLENGE

Every LEGO town should be equipped with a place for LEGO pets to be taken care of! Whether it's dogs, cats or birds, the LEGO vets will take good care of each animal. A man and his dog are waiting to see the vet for an injured paw and a girl is just finishing a checkup with her brand-new puppy! One wall is left open on the building to make the vet's office easier to play with.

KEY ELEMENTS

BUILDING

8—2 x 4 red slopes for the roof
9—2 x 2 red slopes
4—2 x 2 red corner slopes
2—1 x 2 red slopes
8—1 x 2 clear bricks for the window in the examining room
Approximately 200 tan bricks for the building

Door—4 studs wide, 6 bricks high
4 Windows—4 studs wide, 5 bricks high
Chairs, with one 2 x 2 round plate to go under each chair

COMPUTER DESK

2—2 x 6 brown plates
3—2 x 4 plates
1—2 x 2 white plate with one stud
1—chair with a 2 x 2 round plate under it
3—2 x 4 bricks

1—2 x 2 slope with computer screen

EXAMINING TABLE

6—2 x 2 white tiles
8—1 x 1 white bricks
1—4 x 6 tan plate

SHELF

3—2 x 8 plates
10—1 x 2 bricks

The friendly vets quickly put even the most nervous pets at ease.

This vet office is equipped with a comfortable waiting area, a desk for checking in patients and an exam room. Add accessories like coffee mugs and leashes for the dogs.

Boost up each LEGO chair slightly by putting a 2 x 2 round plate underneath. The computer brick is on top of a 2 x 2 plate with one stud on top, which allows the computer to rotate.

This tiny puppy is about to get his first shots! Hopefully he will sit very still and know that the vet is only helping him.

Supplies are kept well organized on the examining room shelf. Stack 1 x 1 round plates to look like containers for medicine and supplies or use round bricks.

The puppy made it through his shots and now he and his owner are on their way to spend the afternoon at the park! That will be a good treat for a well behaved puppy.

PLAYGROUND

NO-INSTRUCTION CREATIVE CHALLENGE

It's a beautiful day and the LEGO minifigures are spending it outside at the playground. This playground is fully functional with a seesaw that moves up and down and a merry-go-round that spins. Add a park bench, a tree and a minifigure walking his dog. Everyone loves to be outdoors on a nice day!

KEY ELEMENTS

PLAY STRUCTURE
Various light gray bricks
Various blue bricks
Various green bricks
2—6 x 10 dark gray plates
1—4 x 8 dark gray plate
Tan plates for the base (size does not have to be exact)
1 x 1 round plates in various colors
1—ladder with clips

MERRY-GO-ROUND
1—6 x 8 plate
1—2 x 2 round plate
1—10 x 10 octagonal plate with hole
1—2 x 2 plate with turntable
4—bars 1 x 4 x 2

SEESAW
1—2 x 10 plate
2—1 x 2 plates
1—4 x 6 plate
1—2 x 2 brick with axles

2—1 x 2 Technic bricks
2—1 x 2 tiles with handle

PARK BENCH
2—2 x 2 light gray bricks
1—2 x 8 dark gray plate
2—1 x 8 dark gray plates
1—2 x 4 light gray plate
2—1 x 4 light gray plates
2—light gray brackets 2 x 2—2 x 2 with two holes

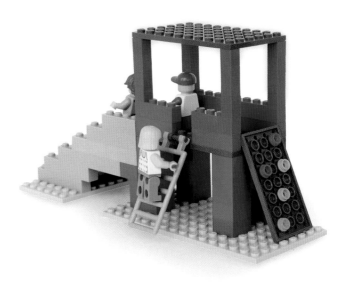

The actual slide is made of a stack of light gray bricks. There are two 1 x 4 light gray bricks, then eight 2 x 4 light gray bricks stacked on top of each other, then one more 1 x 4 brick. It is simply resting against the play structure. A 2 x 4 light gray tile at the bottom keeps the slide in place. Use a 1 x 2 plate with a handle on the side to hold a ladder for the minifigures to climb up. Build the sides of the slide out of light gray bricks.

The other side of the play structure has a rock climbing wall. Use a 4 x 8 plate with colored 1 x 1 round plates for the hand and foot holds.

The merry-go-round is simple to build. Place the 2 x 2 round plate on top of the 2 x 2 turntable and then add the octagonal plate and the bars.

Now the merry-go-round is ready for play!

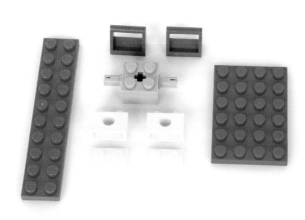

Here are the pieces needed to build the seesaw. Attach the white Technic bricks to the 2 x 2 brick with axle pins. Place a 1 x 2 plate under each Technic brick. (You can make the seesaw swing higher and lower by adding another plate or two under each Technic brick.)

Use brackets (2 x 2—2 x 2) and gray bricks to form the park bench. It tips over easily, but a plate underneath will fix that problem.

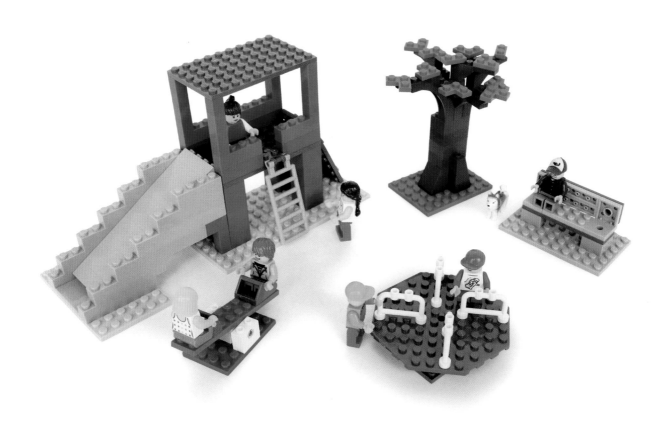

MINIFIGURE FURNITURE FOR LEGO HOUSES

NO-INSTRUCTION CREATIVE CHALLENGE

LEGO minifigures can kick back and relax in this comfortable living room after a busy day at work or play. You can make them rest on the sofa, play video games on the TV and get a bite to eat at the dining table. Accessories like a lamp and a rug transform a pile of bricks into a cozy home. If you're feeling ambitious, you can even create a house with multiple rooms and then furnish it with these projects!

KEY ELEMENTS

SOFA AND CHAIRS
2—4 x 6 dark gray plates
Tan 2 x 4 plates
Various tan bricks

LAMP
1—2 x 2 tan round plate
2—1 x 1 lime green round bricks
1—3 x 3 white disk

END TABLE
1—4 x 4 brown plate
4—1 x 2 brown slopes, inverted
2—2 x 3 brown bricks

1—1 x 4 brown brick

TV CABINET
2—black panels 1 x 2 x 3 bricks high
1—1 x 4 black tile
1—1 x 2 dark gray plate
1—2 x 4 light gray brick
2—brackets 1 x 2—1 x 2
1—1 x 2 grill
1—1 x 1 dark gray round plate
1—1 x 1 translucent red round plate
3—4 x 8 dark gray plates
4—1 x 2 brown slopes, inverted
Various brown bricks

SHELF
3—4 x 6 brown plates
4—1 x 2 brown slopes, inverted
Various brown bricks

DINING TABLE AND CHAIRS
2—dark gray brackets 1 x 2—1 x 2, inverted
2—2 x 2 brown round plates
4—1 x 1 brown round plates
1—4 x 10 brown plate
2—2 x 3 brown plates
8—brown telescopes
8—1 x 1 brown round bricks
4—1 x 1 brown cones

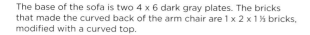

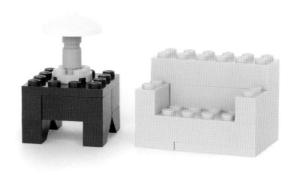

The base of the sofa is two 4 x 6 dark gray plates. The bricks that made the curved back of the arm chair are 1 x 2 x 1⅓ bricks, modified with a curved top.

If you don't have the bricks for the curved arm chair, build this simple chair with tan bricks.

The sides of this cute shelf are made with 1 x 4 bricks modified to look like logs. Use regular brown bricks if you don't have those. Add 1 x 2 bricks in different colors to look like containers on the shelf. Each one has a 1 x 2 tile on the top.

Use a 4 x 8 red plate for the living room rug or substitute something similar.

Build a TV for your minifigures to enjoy.

These are the bricks needed for the TV: one 1 x 4 black tile, one 1 x 2 dark gray plate and two 1 x 2 black panels, three bricks high.

Assemble the TV as shown. If you don't have panels, just use black bricks.

Gather these bricks for the DVD player.

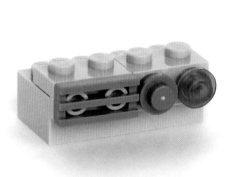

Assemble the DVD player as shown. Isn't it cute?

These LEGO chairs are bar height. If you don't have the telescope bricks or just want to make a lower chair, substitute one 2 x 2 brick for the four telescope bricks on each chair.

The dining room table is a great place to eat pizza together. Use 2 x 2 disks for plates.

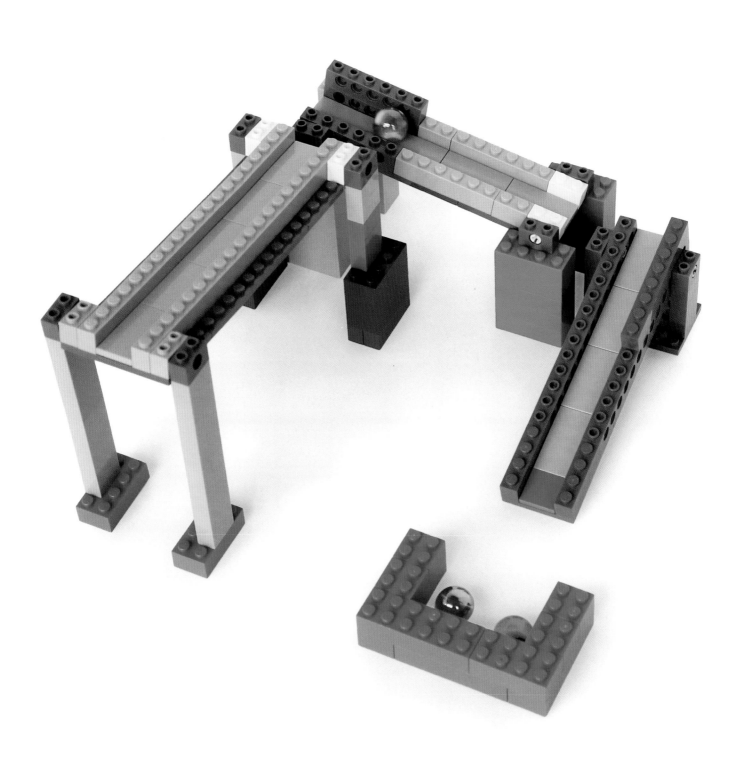

CHAPTER 5

MAKE IT WORK! LEGO CONTRAPTIONS

LEGO bricks are amazing in their versatility. With so many different types of bricks available, it's possible to construct all kinds of contraptions with moving parts. Build a rubber band car that zooms forward under its own power. Create a marble track that can be set up different ways, construct a candy dispenser that actually dispenses a handful of candy and more!

CANDY DISPENSER
STEP-BY-STEP

Fill this candy machine with your favorite candy. Pull the lever on the side of the machine and a handful of candy drops down. Open the door to release the candy into your hand. Simple, fun and YUM! But keep in mind that everyone in the family is going to want to try some of your candy! You might want to stock up! The parts list for this project is flexible, meaning that there are several combinations of bricks that will work.

PARTS LIST

RED BRICKS
2—2 x 4 bricks
6—2 x 6 bricks
7—1 x 6 bricks
2—1 x 8 bricks
4—1 x 4 bricks
6—1 x 2 bricks
1—2 x 10 plate

DARK GRAY BRICKS
2—4 x 4 plates
2—2 x 10 plates
1—2 x 4 plate
2—1 x 6 Technic bricks
2—2 x 2 tiles
1—1 x 2 plate
1—6 x 10 plate

LIGHT GRAY BRICKS
1—2 x 4 tile

1—2 x 4 plate with axles
2—panels 1 x 4 x 1

ASSORTED BRICKS
1—6 x 12 green plate
7—2 x 4 medium blue bricks
4—2 x 2 yellow round bricks
10—1 x 6 yellow bricks or equivalent
4—windows, 4 studs wide and 5 bricks high
1—rocker plate with rocker bearing

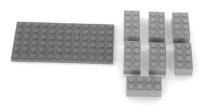

STEP 1: Start by gathering these bricks for the base of the candy dispenser.

STEP 2: Place the medium blue bricks around the edge of the underside of the green plate. Add four 2 x 2 round yellow bricks to make little feet on the machine.

STEP 3: Gather these bricks to make the ramp that the candy will slide down. Place the 2 x 4 tile in the center of the 4 x 4 plate and add the panels on the sides. Attach this to the rocker bearing with rocker plate (hinge).

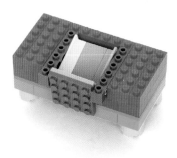

STEP 4: Attach the ramp to the green plate so that one row of studs is visible in front of the ramp.

STEP 5: Add a 2 x 4 red brick on each side of the ramp. Build the door for the candy as shown.

STEP 6: Build up two layers of red bricks around the ramp and door.

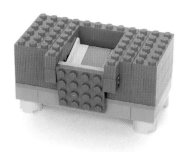

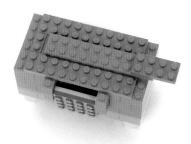

STEP 7: Add a third layer of red bricks. Place a 1 x 6 red brick over each of the Technic bricks that hold the door.

STEP 8: Place two 2 x 10 dark gray plates, two 2 x 2 dark gray tiles and a 1 x 2 plate on the top. The tiles will allow the arm to slide in and out, which will release the candy.

STEP 9: Build the sliding arm with a 2 x 10 red plate and a 2 x 4 gray plate.

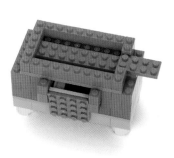

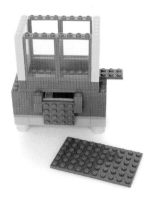

STEP 10: Using bricks that are one stud wide, build one layer around the candy chamber. Be sure to leave an opening for the sliding arm.

STEP 11: Add windows and fill in the sides with yellow bricks.

STEP 12: Fill the candy chamber with candy and place a 6 x 10 dark gray plate on the top as the lid. Your candy machine is ready to go!

ZOOMING MARBLE RUN
NO-INSTRUCTION CREATIVE CHALLENGE

The secret to this zippy marble run is the use of tile bricks on the ramps to create a smooth surface. The structures shown can be arranged in different configurations to create multiple different paths for your marble to zoom down. Experiment with the design until you get it exactly the way you want it. Then make it bigger! How many marble ramps can you build? How high can your design go?

KEY ELEMENTS

At least 10 to 12—1 x 2 Technic bricks with one hole

At least 13—2 x 4 tiles

Technic connector pins

Gray plates

Various bricks to support the ramps

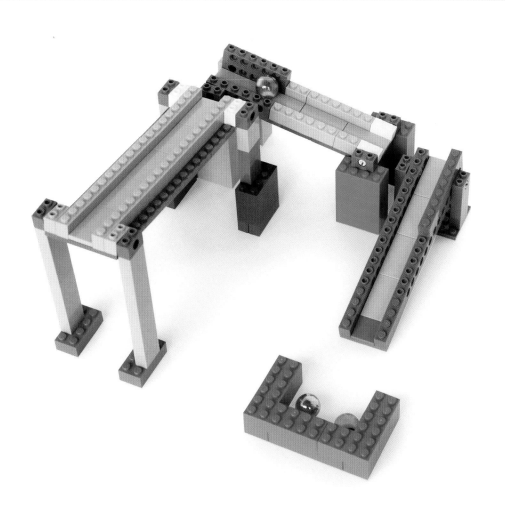

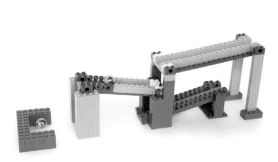

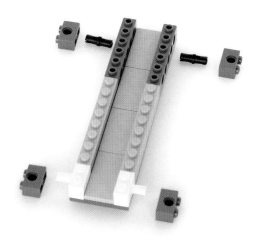

Start the marble at the top and it will roll back and forth down the ramps!

This is the basic design of each ramp. Use Technic connector pins to attach 1 x 2 Technic bricks to the ramp. This allows the ramp to pivot to the angle that you want while the 1 x 2 bricks stay level.

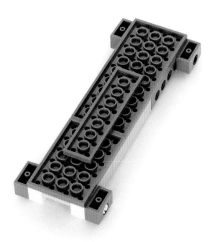

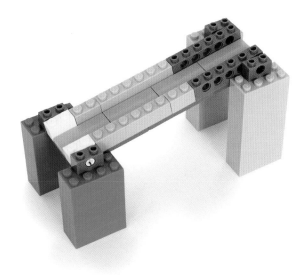

The sections of the ramp are connected with gray plates on the underside. Build the ramps as long as you want them to be!

This is a middle height ramp, designed to sit with both ends on the floor.

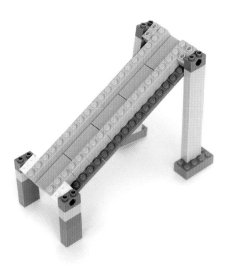

This ramp will have one end on the floor, with the lower end attached to the middle height ramp.

Create one low ramp like this that will take the marble all the way down to the bottom.

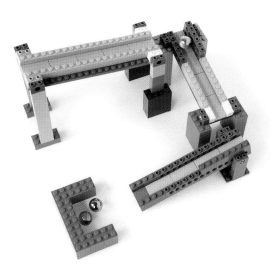

You may have to play with the arrangement of your ramps and the angles of the ramps until you get them in just the right position so that your marble won't fall off.

Here is another way to arrange the ramps. For this configuration, add 1 x 2 bricks to the sides of the ramps in any places where the marble falls off the track. If you get tired of chasing the marbles, you can easily build a box to catch them at the bottom. Two layers of bricks are enough to stop the marbles, even when they are rolling quickly.

Take this project to the next level by adding a task that the marble can perform. For example, you could add a bell at the bottom of the ramp that the marble would ring when it hits it. Or have the marble knock down the first domino in a row of dominoes when it gets to the bottom.

RUBBER BAND POWERED CAR

STEP-BY-STEP

Wind it up and let it go! This simple car will travel across your floor with the power of a single rubber band. To make it go, hook the rubber band around both Technic connector pins. Then turn the back wheels to wind up the rubber band. Set the car down and watch it zoom!

PARTS LIST
1—6 x 10 light gray plate
1—2 x 6 light gray plate
2—1 x 10 light gray bricks
1—2 x 6 light gray brick
2—1 x 8 dark gray bricks

1—2 x 6 Technic plate, with holes
2—1 x 14 Technic bricks (13 holes)
1—Technic axle and pin connector
4—Technic axle pins with friction, length-wise
2—Technic axles, 3 studs long

2—1 x 2 lime green slopes
2—1 x 3 blue slopes
2—large back wheels with x-shaped opening
2—front wheels with x-shaped opening
Rubber band

STEP 1: Gather these bricks for the base of the car.

STEP 2: Build the back wheel assembly. The back axle consists of two Technic axles (3 studs long) and one Technic axle and pin connector. Slide on the two 1 x 14 Technic bricks before adding the rear wheels.

STEP 3: Attach the front wheels to the front hole in each Technic brick. Another option is to use wheels that accept an axle pin instead of an x opening. Then use gray axle pins instead of the pins with the x on one end.

This design allows the axles in the back wheels to turn freely. In other words, the pin that is sticking out turns all the way around as the wheels turn.

STEP 4: Place a 2 x 6 Technic plate with holes two studs away from the front of the car and place a Technic pin in the center hole. This is an important functional element and the rest of the bricks are simply decoration.

To operate the car, loop a rubber band around the front pin and then around the back pin. The rubber band should be long enough to be quite loose around both pins. Then turn the back wheels backwards to wind up the rubber band. In this photo, the 2 x 4 bricks in front of the wheels are holding the car in place. Once the car is wound, it will go zooming off when you let go!

SECRET DRAWER
TREASURE BOX
NO-INSTRUCTION CREATIVE CHALLENGE

This treasure box has a real working drawer, but there's a twist! Anyone who happens upon your treasure box will assume that the handle in front opens the drawer, but that is actually just a decoy. The real drawer is a hidden drawer which opens on the side of the box. Your valuables are safe in this LEGO treasure box!

KEY ELEMENTS

4—6 x 10 light gray plates
1—1 x 2 light gray plate with one stud on top
1—light gray bracket 1 x 2—2 x 2

1—1 x 2 x 1 light gray panel
Various brown bricks
Brown plates for the bottom of the drawer
Brown tiles—to make the drawer slide easily

Anyone who sees this box will think that the drawer opens from the front. But that's a trick!

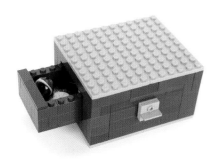

The real drawer actually slides out from the side. Note that the front of the treasure box is constructed to give the appearance of a drawer. In addition to the false handle, the bricks are lined up rather than overlapped to look like the edges of a drawer.

Each side of the box has an opening the exact size of the drawer and the drawer is the same width as the box (12 studs). Open the drawer by pushing on it from either side.

The drawer is 6 studs by 12 studs.

Build supports for the drawer in the bottom of the box. Use brown bricks and cover each brick with a brown tile so that the drawer will slide easily.

Now it's time to assemble the box. Gather your base, your drawer, two light gray plates and extra brown bricks.

Place the drawer in its opening. Then add a layer of bricks on each side of the box between the top of the drawer and the lid. These bricks will just be resting on top of the drawer and then will attach to the lid (gray plates).

Now, what valuable treasures will you keep safe in your secret box?

NINJA ZIP LINE
NO-INSTRUCTION CREATIVE CHALLENGE

This exciting zip line is the perfect addition to any LEGO fort! Make it simple or use a really long string to make the zip line travel all the way across the room. A wheel on the zip line car helps it to travel smoothly down the string.

KEY ELEMENTS

2—1 x 4 dark gray plates
1—1 x 2 dark gray plate with one stud on top

2—1 x 2 dark gray plates with arm up
2—1 x 1 blue bricks
1—1 x 1 light gray brick
1—1 x 2 Technic brick

1—light gray Technic connector pin
2—2 x 2 tiles with lifting ring
1—wheel
String

Build your zip line by tying string to any brick that has a hole in it. The bricks shown are 2 x 2 tiles with a lifting ring.

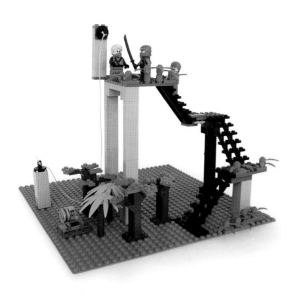

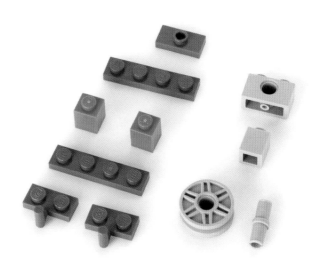

Use ladders and gray plates to create a fort for your minifigures. Add trees and plants for camouflage!

Build a little car with handles for your minifigures to hang on to as they glide down the zip line. A wheel makes the zip line quite fast! Gather these bricks to build it.

Another option is to build a small square car for the minifigure to stand inside. Attach the wheel to the top of the car. Either way, LEGO zip lines are a lot of fun to play with!

CHAPTER 6

WILD ANIMALS

LEGO animals are fun to build and round tile eyes give them great personality. When designing a LEGO animal, it helps to look at a picture of the actual animal while building. Pay attention to the structure of the animal's body. For example, does the animal have eyes that face forward or are the eyes on the side of the head? How long is the animal's body compared to its head? How do its legs move and how are they attached to the body? Build a friendly rhino, a mischievous monkey and more in this chapter full of creature creations! Then build a habitat for your animal to live in. Construct trees, bushes and rocks. Use blue bricks to build a pond or a river. Your LEGO animals will seem to come to life in their environment!

MONKEY
STEP-BY-STEP

What makes a monkey a monkey? Its tail! Although monkeys are similar to apes, monkeys have tails and apes do not. Many monkeys have tails that are prehensile, meaning that they can bend their tail in order to use it like an extra hand. This fun LEGO monkey is ready to climb some trees and swing through the jungle!

PARTS LIST

BROWN BRICKS
2—2 x 4 plates
3—1 x 2 plates
3—1 x 4 plates
6—2 x 3 plates
2—1 x 2 plates with one stud on top
6—1 x 3 plates
4—1 x 1 bricks

5—1 x 4 bricks
5—2 x 2 bricks
4—1 x 2 bricks
4—2 x 4 bricks
3—2 x 2 slopes, inverted
2—1 x 2 slopes, inverted
4—2 x 2 slopes
4—1 x 1 slopes, 30 degree
2—2 x 2 round plates

TAN BRICKS
2—1 x 2 bricks
1—2 x 4 plate
2—1 x 1 bricks with one stud on the side
1—1 x 2 plate with one stud on top
1—1 x 2 plate

BLACK BRICKS
1—1 x 1 round plate
2—eyes

STEP 1: Gather these bricks for the head.

STEP 2: Build the nose and face as shown.

STEP 3: Attach the eyes to the 1 x 1 tan bricks with one stud and find a 1 x 2 tan plate.

STEP 4: Place the 1 x 2 tan plate just behind the nose and place the eyes directly on top of that. Build the ears and the top of the head as shown.

STEP 5: Add the ears to the head just behind the eyes.

STEP 6: Turn the head over and add one 2 x 2 brown inverted slope and two 1 x 2 brown inverted slopes.

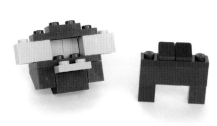

STEP 7: Build the back of the head as shown.

STEP 8: Attach the back of the head. Place a 1 x 2 brown plate on top of a 2 x 2 brown brick and attach this under the tan plate on the back of the head.

STEP 9: Add a 1 x 2 brown plate above the eyes and two 1 x 1 brown slopes on the sides of the face.

STEP 10: Start building the body. Find two 2 x 3 brown plates (or a 2 x 6 plate) and a 1 x 4 brown plate.

STEP 11: Add two 2 x 3 brown plates so that they connect the plates from step 10. Place a 2 x 4 brown plate on top of that. Then add a 1 x 2 brown plate with one stud on top.

STEP 12: Build the body as shown.

STEP 13: Add two 2 x 2 brown inverted slopes and two 1 x 3 brown plates to the underside of the body.

STEP 14: Build the arms, legs and tail as shown.

STEP 15: Attach a 1 x 2 brown plate with one stud on top to the plates that stick out from the back of the body. Attach the tail to this.

STEP 16: Attach the head to the body and the monkey is ready to explore the jungle!

ELEPHANT

NO-INSTRUCTION CREATIVE CHALLENGE

Elephants are fascinating creatures and the world's largest land animals. They may look funny with their long trunks and huge ears, but there are good reasons for both of these body parts. Elephant's ears help to regulate their body temperature and their trunks are used for breathing, lifting water to their mouths, smelling, trumpeting and even moving objects. It's pretty amazing that elephants can do all that with their noses! This LEGO elephant is designed to look like an African elephant with it's large ears and head. Asian elephants have flatter foreheads and smaller ears and they are smaller overall.

KEY ELEMENTS

Various dark gray bricks and plates
8—1 x 1 white round plates for the toenails
4—2 x 2 dark gray plates for the bottoms
    of the feet

EARS
2—1 x 3 dark gray slopes
2—1 x 2 slopes, inverted
4—1 x 2 bricks

TRUNK AND TUSKS
1—2 x 3 dark gray plate

6—1 x 2 dark gray bricks
4—1 x 1 white round bricks

TAIL
1—dark gray bracket 1 x 2—2 x 2
1—1 x 2 plate with one stud on top
1—1 x 6 dark gray plate

Using these pictures as a guide, see if you can design your own LEGO elephant.

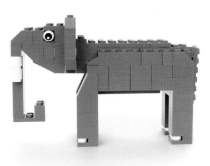

Build the shape of the elephant's head by using a row of 2 x 2 inverted slopes and then a row of 2 x 3 inverted slopes.

Each ear is made up of one 1 x 3 slope, two 1 x 2 bricks and one 1 x 2 inverted slope. The trunk has five 1 x 2 bricks, a 2 x 3 plate and one more 1 x 2 brick on the curved part of the trunk. Or use 1 x 2 bricks that are two or four bricks high.

Attach the tail by using a 1 x 2—2 x 2 bracket and a 1 x 2 plate with one stud on top. The 1 x 2 plates with one stud are so useful for centering bricks. This brick allows the tail to be right in the middle of the bracket rather than on one side or the other.

Build a habitat for your elephant by assembling some trees and bushes. Elephants are known to travel long distances for water. You might want to try building a pond for your elephant!

LION
STEP-BY-STEP

Lions are beautiful and fascinating wild cats. They are the second largest wild cats and the only wild cats to live in groups, which are called prides. The female lion does most of the hunting, bringing down primarily antelope, zebra and wildebeest. This LEGO design captures the lion's personality and the strength of his legs. Modify this design to make a female lion by removing the mane, building up the head with yellow bricks and adding yellow 1 x 2 bricks as ears.

PARTS LIST

YELLOW BRICKS
3—2 x 4 plates
8—2 x 2 plates
3—1 x 4 plates
1—4 x 6 plate
2—2 x 2 bricks
2—1 x 1 bricks with a stud on the side

3—1 x 4 bricks
10—1 x 2 bricks
6—2 x 4 bricks
2—2 x 3 bricks with a curved end

BROWN BRICKS
6—1 x 2 bricks
2—1 x 1 bricks
2—1 x 4 bricks

2—2 x 2 bricks
3—2 x 2 slopes, inverted
4—1 x 1 slopes, 30 degree

ASSORTED BRICKS
2—eyes
1—1 x 2 black plate

STEP 1: Gather these bricks for the lion's head.

STEP 2: Stack the bricks as shown.

STEP 3: Add the eyes and a 2 x 2 yellow brick between them.

STEP 4: Find the four bricks shown. Attach the stacked 1 x 4 yellow and 2 x 2 yellow bricks under the 2 x 2 yellow brick between the eyes.

STEP 5: Add the two plates shown in step 4 on the top of the head.

STEP 6: Build the sides of the mane. The sides should be mirror images of each other.

STEP 7: Attach the sides of the mane to the head. Note that they attach under the head. Add one 2 x 2 brown inverted slope under the chin and two 2 x 2 brown bricks on the top of the head.

STEP 8: Gather these bricks for the body.

STEP 9: Attach the bricks on top of the 4 x 6 yellow plate.

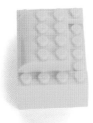

STEP 10: Add one 1 x 4 yellow plate on each side.

STEP 11: Add two 2 x 3 yellow bricks with a curved end. If you don't have those, use regular 2 x 3 yellow bricks.

STEP 12: Line up a 2 x 4 yellow plate and two 2 x 2 yellow plates as shown.

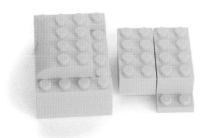

STEP 13: Connect them with two 2 x 4 yellow bricks.

STEP 14: Using two more 2 x 4 yellow bricks, connect the two parts of the body as shown.

STEP 15: Add one 1 x 2 yellow brick to each side. This will be the top of the front legs.

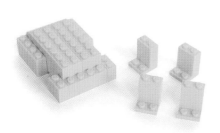

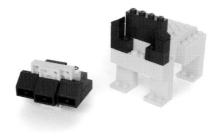

STEP 16: Build the legs. Each leg has two 1 x 2 yellow bricks and a 2 x 2 yellow plate for the foot.

STEP 17: Attach the legs to the body. Build up the back of the mane on the body.

STEP 18: Attach the head and the lion is complete!

TOUCAN
NO-INSTRUCTION CREATIVE CHALLENGE

Toucans are fascinating birds with their long, colorful beaks. A toucan's beak is roughly one third of its body length! What does a toucan need a long beak for? Scientists aren't completely sure, but the enormous beak may actually help a toucan stay cool during hot weather. This colorful LEGO toucan is ready to fly through the jungle!

KEY ELEMENTS

2—1 x 1 yellow bricks with a stud on the side to hold the eyes
Various black, orange and white bricks

1—2 x 2 white slope, inverted, for the neck
2—1 x 3 orange curved slopes for the beak
2—eyes

Use these pictures as a guide and see if you can figure out how to build the toucan. He is only one layer wide, meaning that all of the bricks used are visible.

Use a 1 x 4 black plate and two 1 x 2 black plates to build the toucan's feet.

PARROT
NO-INSTRUCTION CREATIVE CHALLENGE

Parrots are tropical birds that are known for their beautiful colors and their tremendous noise. In fact, some parrots can repeat human speech, and trained parrots can answer questions and even count. Pretty amazing for a bird! This LEGO parrot is designed after the blue-and-yellow macaw, one of the largest types of parrot. See if you can build this colorful parrot using just the photos. Tropical birds are very colorful and you can substitute different colors wherever you need to.

KEY ELEMENTS

2—2 x 2 yellow plates
2—1 x 3 yellow plates
2—1 x 2 yellow tiles
1—1 x 2 yellow brick
1—1 x 2 yellow slope, 30 degree
1—2 x 2 yellow slope, inverted

1—2 x 2 blue slope
1—1 x 2 white brick
2—1 x 1 green bricks with a stud on the side
1—1 x 2 green plate with one stud on top
2—1 x 6 aqua plates
1—1 x 2 aqua brick

1—2 x 2 aqua slope, inverted
1—2 x 3 turquoise slope
1—1 x 2 turquoise brick
1—2 x 2 dark gray plate
2—1 x 1 dark gray round plates
1—1 x 2 black plate
2—eyes

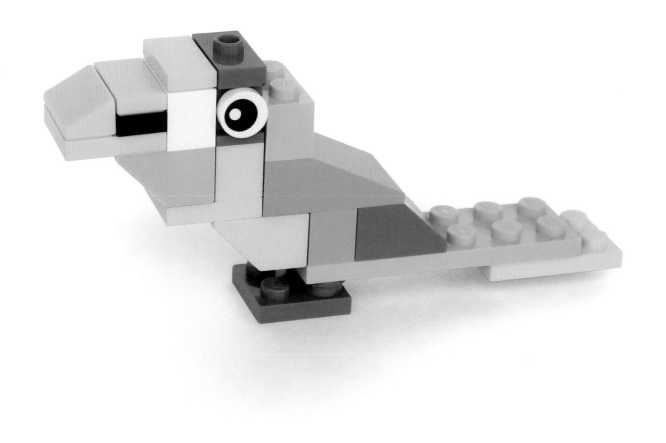

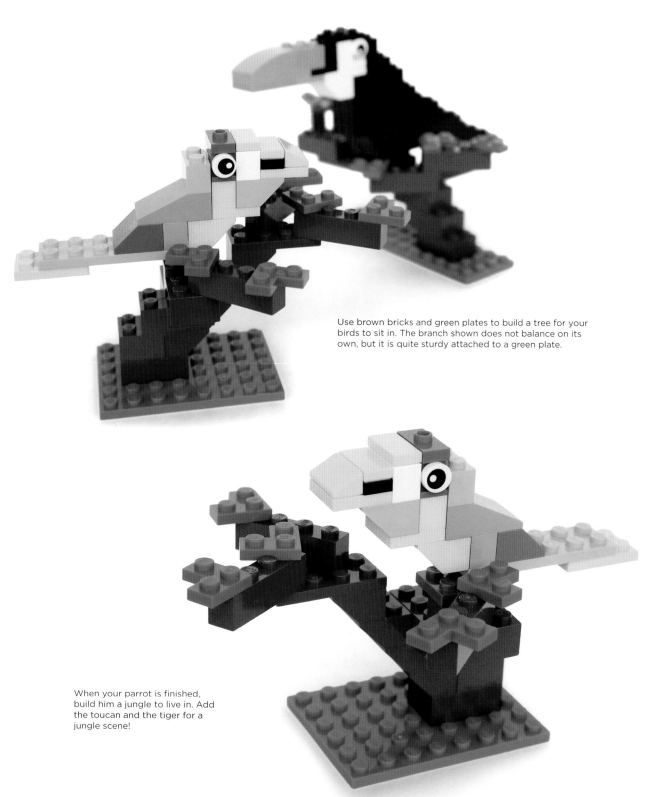

Use brown bricks and green plates to build a tree for your birds to sit in. The branch shown does not balance on its own, but it is quite sturdy attached to a green plate.

When your parrot is finished, build him a jungle to live in. Add the toucan and the tiger for a jungle scene!

TIGER
STEP-BY-STEP

The sleek and stealthy tiger is the largest wild cat in the world, weighing in at an impressive 600 pounds or more. Tigers are generally solitary creatures and hunt alone. They are capable of using their strong and powerful teeth to bring down large prey that are more than twice the tiger's weight. Their stripes serve as camouflage and no two tigers have exactly the same stripe pattern. This LEGO tiger may not look like a fierce hunter, but don't let his adorable looks fool you!

PARTS LIST

ORANGE BRICKS
2—2 x 4 bricks
9—2 x 2 bricks
5—1 x 4 bricks
2—1 x 2 bricks
5—1 x 2 plates
1—2 x 3 plate
1—1 x 2 plate with one stud on top
1—2 x 3 wedge plate, right
1—2 x 3 wedge plate, left
2—2 x 2 slopes

2—1 x 2 slopes
1—2 x 2 slope, inverted
1—2 x 3 slope, inverted
2—1 x 3 curved slopes
1—bracket 1 x 2—2 x 2

BLACK BRICKS
7—1 x 2 plates
4—2 x 3 plates
4—2 x 2 plates
6—1 x 4 bricks
1—1 x 4 tile or plate
2—antennas

WHITE BRICKS
1—1 x 4 plate
1—4 x 8 plate
1—4 x 4 plate
2—2 x 4 plates
1—2 x 2 plate modified with one stud on top
2—1 x 1 bricks with one stud on the side
3—2 x 4 bricks
1—1 x 2 brick
2 eyes

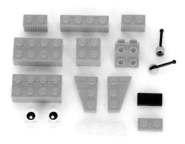

STEP 1: Gather the bricks shown for the tiger's face.

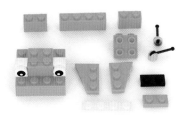

STEP 2: Connect two 2 x 4 orange bricks with a 2 x 2 orange brick. Add the 1 x 1 white bricks with a stud on the side and attach the eyes.

STEP 3: Add the orange bracket and a 1 x 2 black plate for the nose. Add two 1 x 2 orange bricks for the ears and a 1 x 4 orange brick behind the ears.

STEP 4: Add the orange wedge plate bricks to the top of the head and the antennas for whiskers. Attach the white 1 x 4 plate under the nose to become the chin. Attach the 1 x 2 orange plate under that.

STEP 5: Find a 4 x 4 white plate and a 4 x 8 white plate for the base of the body.

STEP 6: Build stripes onto the body as shown. Each stripe is a 1 x 4 (orange or black) brick with a 1 x 2 (orange or black) plate on top.

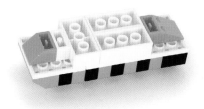

STEP 7: Turn the tiger upside down and build the belly as shown.

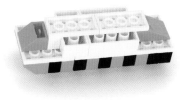

STEP 8: Add two white 2 x 4 plates to the belly.

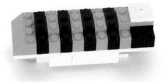

STEP 9: Turn the body over again. Add an orange 2 x 3 plate and a white 2 x 2 plate with one stud on top. This will allow the tiger's head to turn.

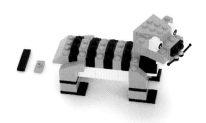

STEP 10: Build the legs as shown.

STEP 11: Attach the body to the legs as shown. Find a 1 x 2 orange plate with one stud and a 1 x 4 black tile or plate for the tail.

STEP 12: Attach the tail as shown.

Your tiger is ready to explore the jungle!

WALRUS
STEP-BY-STEP

The walrus is a marine mammal with large flippers that is native to the Arctic Circle. How do walruses stay warm in such a frigid climate? With lots and lots of body fat! Walruses are known for being noisy creatures and for their tusks, which can grow up to 3 feet long and weigh up to 12 pounds each. This friendly walrus is ready to swim! Build him an icy pool and he'll be ready to explore!

PARTS LIST

BROWN BRICKS

2—4 x 4 plates
2—1 x 4 plates
5—2 x 4 plates
3—1 x 2 plates
2—1 x 2 plates with one stud on the top
6—1 x 2 bricks

3—2 x 4 bricks
1—1 x 4 brick
2—1 x 1 bricks
2—1 x 1 bricks with a stud on the side
3—2 x 2 slopes
2—2 x 4 slopes
3—2 x 2 slopes, inverted
4—1 x 1 slopes, 30 degree
1—1 x 2 tile

ASSORTED BRICKS

1—1 x 2 black plate with one stud on the top
2—1 x 1 white cones
2—eyes

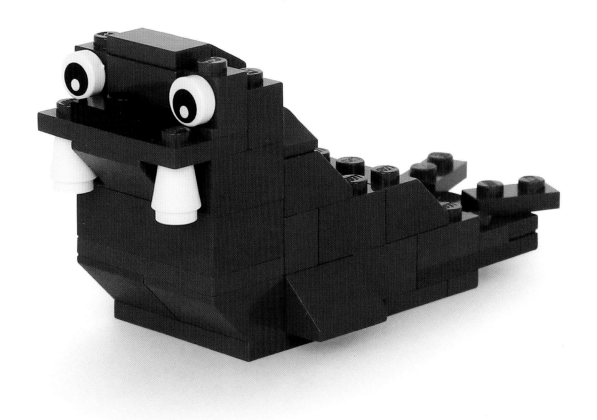

STEP 1: Start with a 4 x 4 brown plate, a 2 x 4 brown plate and a 1 x 4 brown plate.

STEP 2: Add two 2 x 2 brown slopes, two 2 x 2 brown inverted slopes, one 2 x 4 brown brick and two 1 x 2 brown bricks.

STEP 3: Add a 4 x 4 brown plate on the back and add a 2 x 4 brown plate over the two inverted slopes on the front of the walrus.

STEP 4: Add a 1 x 4 brown plate and two 2 x 4 brown plates (stacked) on the back.

STEP 5: From back to front, add a 2 x 4 brown slope, a 2 x 4 brown brick, a 1 x 4 brown brick and another 2 x 4 brown brick.

STEP 6: Build up the head as shown.

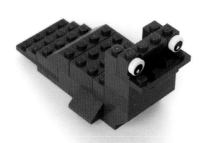

STEP 7: Add a 2 x 4 plate to the front of the head. Add the eyes with a 1 x 2 brick between them and the black 1 x 2 plate for the nose.

STEP 8: Turn the walrus around. Add a 1 x 2 brown brick, a 2 x 4 brown slope and a 1 x 2 brown plate behind the head. Then find the bricks shown next to the walrus.

STEP 9: Place a 2 x 2 brown slope behind the head and add the four 1 x 1 brown slopes as shown. Place a 1 x 2 brown tile on the top of the head and build the back flippers.

STEP 10: Add two 1 x 1 white cone bricks for the tusks and the walrus is complete!

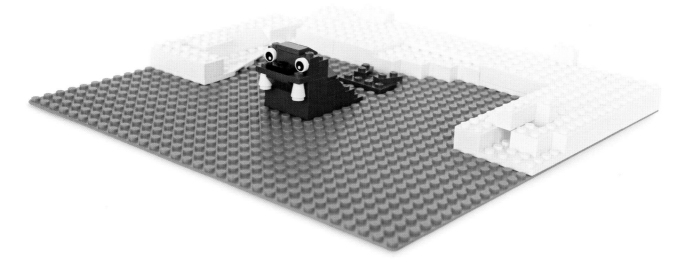

Build your walrus an icy ocean to swim in! Make him look like he is really in the water by removing the bottom half of his body. Add some LEGO fish for him to catch!

RHINOCEROS
STEP-BY-STEP

The rhinoceros is the second largest land animal in the world, smaller only than the elephant. Because of their massive size and their tough skin, rhinos have few natural enemies. There are five different species of rhino and the white rhino is the largest species, with the males weighing in at about 5,000 pounds. Despite their weight, white rhinos are surprisingly fast and can run at speeds close to 30 mph. With its detailed and realistic look, this LEGO rhino is ready to thunder across the African savannah!

PARTS LIST

LIGHT GRAY BRICKS
3—4 x 4 plates
1—2 x 3 plate
1—1 x 4 plate
1—6 x 10 plate
2—1 x 2 plates with one stud on top
1—1 x 1 round plate
1—1 x 2 plate with clips on the side
1—1 x 2 plate with a handle on the side

1—2 x 3 brick
2—1 x 3 bricks
14—2 x 2 bricks
1—1 x 4 brick
3—1 x 1 bricks
12—1 x 2 bricks
4—1 x 1 bricks with a stud on the side
2—2 x 8 bricks
1—2 x 6 brick
6—1 x 1 slopes, 30 degree

4—2 x 4 slopes
6—2 x 2 slopes
2—1 x 2 slopes
10—2 x 2 slopes, inverted
2—1 x 2 slopes, inverted
1—2 x 3 brick with a curved end

ASSORTED BRICKS
2—eyes
4—2 x 3 dark gray plates

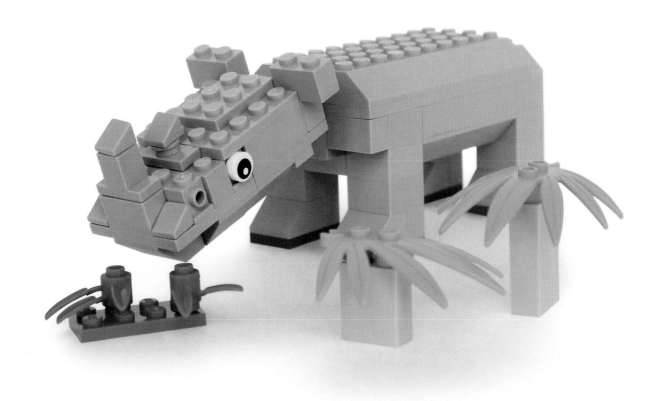

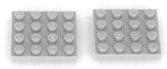

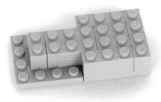

STEP 1: Begin the head with two 4 x 4 plates.

STEP 2: Add light gray bricks as shown.

STEP 3: In the open space on each side, add a 1 x 1 light gray brick, a 1 x 1 light gray brick with a stud on the side, an eye and a 1 x 1 light gray slope. Add a 1 x 2 light gray brick to the front of the face.

STEP 4: Add a 4 x 4 light gray plate, leaving one row of studs uncovered at the back of the head. Add a 2 x 3 light gray plate and two 1 x 2 light gray plates with one stud on top.

STEP 5: Finish the head by adding 1 x 2 light gray bricks as ears, two 1 x 1 light gray slopes between the ears and horns. The front horn is a 1 x 1 light gray brick and a 1 x 1 light gray slope. The second horn is a 1 x 1 light gray round plate and a 1 x 1 light gray slope.

STEP 6: Turn the head over and add five 2 x 2 light gray inverted slopes, a 1 x 4 light gray plate and a 1 x 2 plate with clips.

STEP 7: Build the rhino's body. On the underside of a 6 x 10 light gray plate, add the bricks shown.

STEP 8: Place the 1 x 2 light gray plate with a handle and the 1 x 2 light gray brick on the end of the 6 x 10 light gray plate. This will hold the rhino's head.

STEP 9: Turn the body over. The photo shows the body turned so that the head end now faces the left. Add four 2 x 4 light gray slopes, two 2 x 2 light gray slopes, a 2 x 8 light gray brick (or two 2 x 4 bricks) and a 2 x 3 light gray brick with a curved end.

STEP 10: Turn the body upside down again and add the bricks shown.

STEP 11: Build the legs. Each front leg is made up of a 2 x 3 dark gray plate, a 2 x 2 slope, a 1 x 2 brick and two 2 x 2 bricks. Each back leg has the same foot but with an extra 2 x 2 brick and a 1 x 2 slope on top.

STEP 12: Attach the head and legs to the body and the rhino is complete! Build him a habitat with some bushes and a little pond. Then send your minifigures on a safari to observe some wild animals!

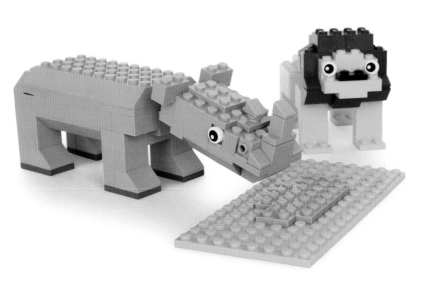

ALLIGATOR AND TURTLE

NO-INSTRUCTION CREATIVE CHALLENGE

These two LEGO reptiles are the perfect creatures to round out your LEGO zoo. Build an alligator with a mouthful of teeth and an adorable little turtle. The alligator might be much larger than the turtle, but did you know that both creatures eat meat? For turtles, the amount of meat depends on the species. Most semi-aquatic turtles eat mainly meat, while tortoises eat mostly plants.

KEY ELEMENTS

TURTLE

1—4 x 6 tan plate
1—2 x 4 tan plate
4—2 x 2 tan slopes
4—1 x 1 tan slopes, 30 degree
1—1 x 2 green plate with a handle on the side

1—1 x 2 green plate with clips on the side
2—2 x 3 green plates
2—1 x 2 green bricks
2—1 x 1 green bricks with a stud on the side
4—1 x 1 green bricks
2—eyes

ALLIGATOR

2 x 4 green plates
2—1 x 1 green bricks with a stud on the side
Green bricks
8—1 x 2 curved slopes for the legs
6—1 x 1 white round plates for the teeth
2—eyes

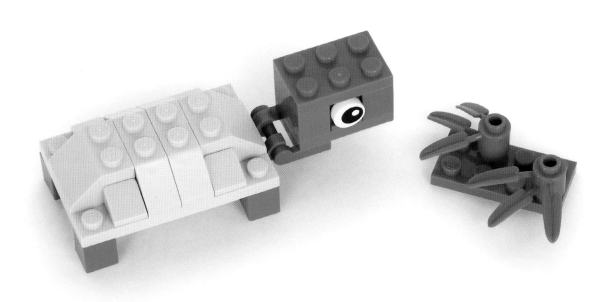

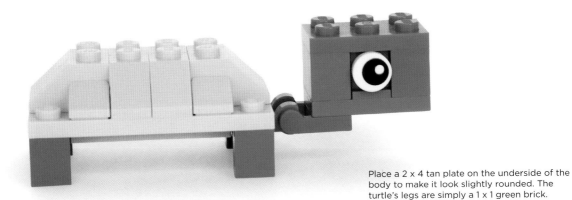

Place a 2 x 4 tan plate on the underside of the body to make it look slightly rounded. The turtle's legs are simply a 1 x 1 green brick.

This adorable turtle has a head that moves up and down. It would be fun to make the turtle a tiny pet! Build an aquarium for him to live in or a shallow cage. Add a food dish and some rocks for him to climb on.

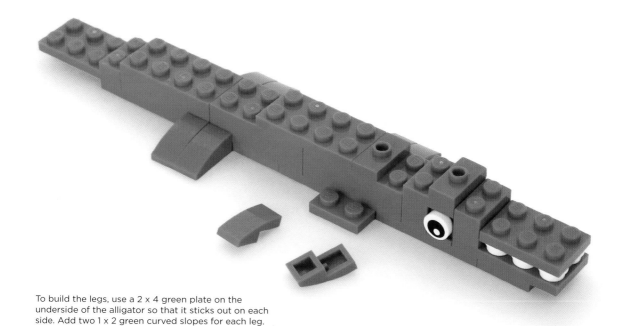

To build the legs, use a 2 x 4 green plate on the underside of the alligator so that it sticks out on each side. Add two 1 x 2 green curved slopes for each leg.

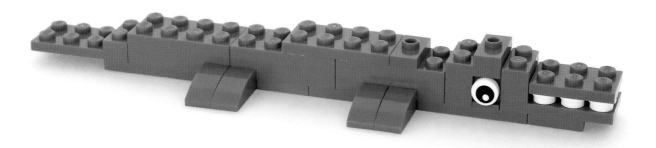

Build a river or a swamp for your aligator to live in. Your minifigures can go out on a boat to look for alligators. But make sure they don't get too close!

CHAPTER 7

BUILD AND PLAY! LEGO GAMES

Give traditional games new life by building them out of LEGO bricks! Or invent your own board game with your own rules—and it doesn't have to be flat, either. Create a board game that travels through a fort and over a mountain. Build your own chess set with custom game pieces. Build a puzzle for someone else to solve. Game night is more fun with LEGO!

TABLE TOP FOOSBALL GAME

NO-INSTRUCTION CREATIVE CHALLENGE

Foosball, also known as table soccer, is a fun and fast-paced game! Players compete to kick a ball into the goal. This miniature version built out of LEGO bricks can be played on a table top with a marble as the ball. Start the game by dropping the marble in the center of the playing field. The game continues until one player has scored 10 goals.

SPECIFICATIONS

- The game is built on two 32 x 32 stud base plates.
- The overall dimensions of the game are 47 studs by 26 studs.
- Each goal is 4 studs by 8 studs and sticks out past the 47 stud length.
- Each team has three rods.
- The goalie rod has two players and the other two rods have three players each.

KEY ELEMENTS

Red and blue bricks for the walls of the game (color is not important)

Dark gray plates for the top layer

Red bricks (one stud wide) for the goals

8—red Technic liftarms, 2 x 4 L-shaped thick

15—red Technic axle connectors, smooth, x-shaped hole + orientation

3—light gray Technic axle connectors, smooth, x-shaped hole + orientation

8—light gray Technic liftarms, 2 x 4 L-shaped thick

115—2 x 4 light gray tiles
2—1 x 2 light gray tiles
3—1 x 6 light gray tiles
1—1 x 4 light gray tile
6—2 x 2 white tiles
12—1 x 2 dark gray Technic bricks
10—Technic axles, 12 studs long
8—Technic axles, 10 studs long

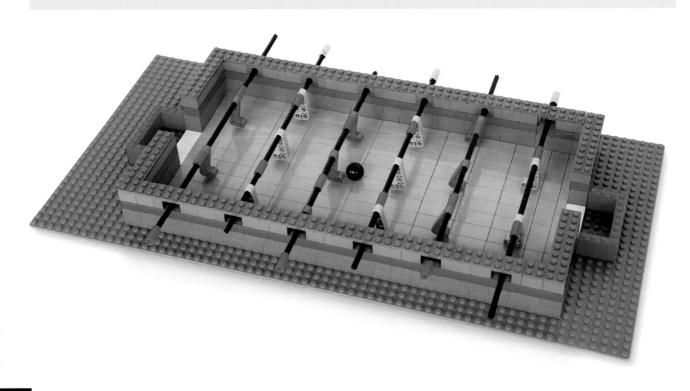

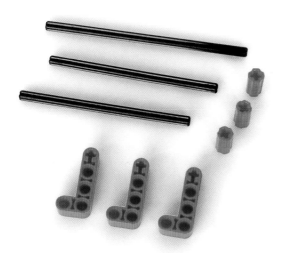

Each team will have two rods made up of two 10 stud Technic axles, one 12 stud Technic axle, three connectors and three L-shaped liftarms. Each team will also have a goalie rod made up of three 12 stud Technic axles, three connectors and two L-shaped liftarms.

The L-shaped liftarms have an x-shaped opening that slides onto the Technic axles. They fit snugly and do not spin when you spin the rod, which makes them sturdy enough to hit the ball.

After building each rod, slide each end through a 1 x 2 Technic brick. These Technic bricks will attach to the game table. The goalie rods are placed 3 studs from the end of the field. Then there are 5 studs between each of the 1 x 2 Technic bricks. The spacing was determined by the best possible reach of each player on the field so that the ball will not get stuck during game play.

CHECKERS

NO-INSTRUCTION CREATIVE CHALLENGE

Build your own checkers game! This classic game is fun to play with a friend. A standard LEGO baseplate (32 studs by 32 studs) works perfectly for a checker board. Use 4 x 4 plates to create the squares on the board. Create your game with the colors shown or choose your own colors!

KEY ELEMENTS

CHECKER BOARD

1—tan base plate
32—4 x 4 tan plates
32—4 x 4 red plates

GAME PIECES

12—2 x 2 blue bricks
6—1 x 1 blue bricks (optional)
12—2 x 2 yellow bricks
6—1 x 1 yellow bricks (optional)

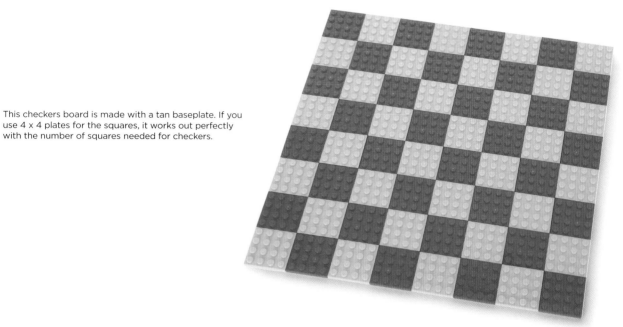

This checkers board is made with a tan baseplate. If you use 4 x 4 plates for the squares, it works out perfectly with the number of squares needed for checkers.

Line up 12 bricks on each side and play according the the rules for checkers. There are a couple of options for marking pieces that have become kings. Either stack two 2 x 2 bricks using pieces that have been captured in game play or add a 1 x 1 brick to the kings.

CHESS

NO-INSTRUCTION CREATIVE CHALLENGE

Use LEGO bricks to create your own chess set! In addition to being a great game of strategy, chess is interesting because of the great variety of unique chess sets. This LEGO chess set will be a fun addition to your game collection! Refer to the checkers game on page 148 for details on how to build the game board.

PARTS LIST

Checkers game board (see page 148)

PAWNS (8 PER SIDE)
8—2 x 2 black bricks
8—1 x 1 black cones
8—2 x 2 white bricks
8—1 x 1 white cones

KNIGHTS (2 PER SIDE)
2—2 x 2 black bricks
2—1 x 1 black bricks
2—1 x 2 black bricks
2—1 x 2 black plates with one stud on top
4—1 x 1 black slopes, 30 degree
2—2 x 2 white bricks
2—1 x 1 white bricks
2—1 x 2 white bricks
2—1 x 2 white plates with one stud on top
4—1 x 1 white slopes, 30 degree

ROOKS (2 PER SIDE)
2—black 2 x 2 bricks

4—1 x 1 black round bricks
4—2 x 2 black plates
8—1 x 1 black slopes, 30 degree
2—2 x 2 white bricks
4—1 x 1 white round bricks
4—2 x 2 white plates
8—1 x 1 white slopes, 30 degree

BISHOPS (2 PER SIDE)
2—2 x 2 black bricks
4—1 x 1 black bricks
2—2 x 2 black plates with one stud on top
2—2 x 2 black round plates
2—1 x 1 black cones
2—2 x 2 black disks
2—2 x 2 white bricks
4—1 x 1 white bricks
2—2 x 2 white plates with one stud on top
2—2 x 2 white round plates
2—1 x 1 white cones
2—2 x 2 white disks

QUEEN (1 PER SIDE)
4—2 x 2 black bricks
2—2 x 2 black slopes, inverted
2—1 x 2 black slopes
1—1 x 2 black slope, 45 degree triple
4—2 x 2 white bricks
2—2 x 2 white slopes, inverted
2—1 x 2 white slopes
1—1 x 2 white slope, triple

KING (1 PER SIDE)
4—2 x 2 black bricks
3—1 x 2 black bricks
1—2 x 2 black plate
1—1 x 2 black slope, 45 degree triple
1—2 x 4 black slope, inverted double
4—2 x 2 white bricks
3—1 x 2 white bricks
1—2 x 2 white plate
1—1 x 2 white slope, 45 degree triple
1—2 x 4 white slope, inverted double

The pawns are simple to build with a 2 x 2 brick and a 1 x 1 cone each.

The knight is designed to look like a simple horse. For each knight, place a 1 x 2 plate with one stud on top of a 2 x 2 brick. Add a 1 x 1 brick, a 1 x 2 brick and two 1 x 1 slopes.

Each rook has a 2 x 2 brick, a 1 x 1 round brick, a 2 x 2 plate and another 1 x 1 round brick. The top is a 2 x 2 plate decorated with four 1 x 1 slopes.

1 x 2 triple slope bricks give the king and queen a distinct royal look. To build the king (shown on the left), stack four 2 x 2 bricks. Then add a 2 x 2 plate. The top of the king is a 2 x 4 double inverted slope, three 1 x 2 bricks and a 1 x 2 triple slope. To build the queen (shown on the right), stack four 2 x 2 bricks. Add two 2 x 2 inverted slopes on top of that. Then place two 1 x 2 slope bricks and a 1 x 2 triple slope on the top.

The bishop looks like a simple tower. Start with a 2 x 2 brick. Add a 2 x 2 plate with one stud on top, then two 1 x 1 bricks. The top is a 2 x 2 round plate, a 1 x 1 cone and a 2 x 2 disk.

NINJA QUEST BOARD GAME

NO-INSTRUCTION CREATIVE CHALLENGE

This Ninja Quest game combines LEGO ninja minifigures with an adventure board game. The great thing about building a LEGO game is that you can determine what the game board will look like and you can decide on your own rules. Use our board game idea or create your own!

KEY ELEMENTS

2—tan base plates

2 x 4 green, lime green, blue, dark red and orange plates

4—Ninja minifigures

1—die

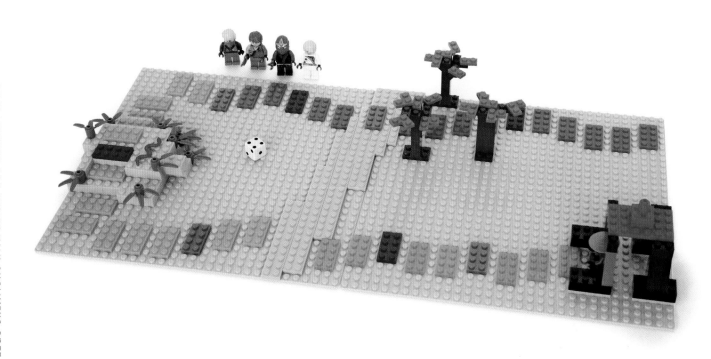

RULES OF THE GAME

1. On their turn, each player rolls the die and moves that number of spaces.
2. The dark red spaces are battle squares. If a player lands on a battle square, he and one opponent on the game board each roll the die. The opponent is the closest player on the board, whether ahead or behind the player who landed on the battle square. The player who rolls the higher number either keeps the more advanced position on the board if he was ahead or moves to the more advanced position on the board if he was behind.
3. The blue spaces are ninja challenge squares. If a player lands on a blue space, he has to perform a ninja challenge. Get creative! Some ideas for the challenges are to do 10 sit-ups, perform an imaginary ninja duel or sneak down a hallway. Or make the challenges something that the minifigures will do.
4. The player who arrives at the Ninja Master Dojo first is the winner!

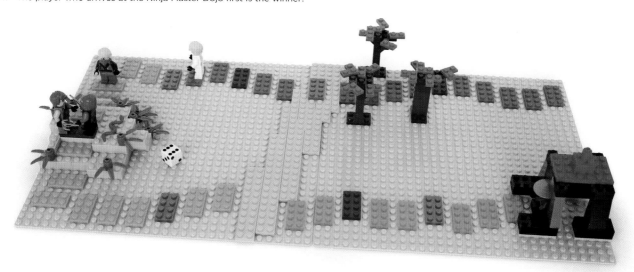

IDEAS FOR EXTENDING THE GAME

1. Create a challenge for entering the Ninja Master Dojo. For example, players have to roll a certain number before they can gain entrance to the dojo and win the game.
2. Add ninja fact cards. Create spaces on the game board that require players to draw a card and answer a question.
3. Add more dimensions to your game board. Make the players travel up over a mountain, for example.

AMAZING SPINNING TOPS
NO-INSTRUCTION CREATIVE CHALLENGE

Build some LEGO tops that spin well and spin fast! Once you try building these tops, you'll want to keep creating more. It's fun to modify the tops with different colors and designs. It's also fun to try battling the tops against each other. Find some friends and a smooth playing surface. Spin your tops and see whose top can knock the other tops over!

KEY ELEMENTS

2 x 2 round plates
1 x 1 round plates in all colors
1 x 1 cones

2 x 2 round bricks
Round plates with a hole in the middle
Technic axles
Technic connector pins, ½ length

One thing that you will quickly discover when building tops is that the center of gravity needs to be close to the ground. In other words, your top will need to have only a small amount of axle sticking out on the bottom or it won't spin properly.

The first way to build a top is to use a round plate with a hole in the center. Slide a Technic axle through the hole, but it won't be secure. Add a 2 x 2 round plate to the bottom of the top as shown on the left. This will hold the axle in place.

Another way to build a top is to use a Technic connector pin—the short half-length version. Add one of these to the bottom of a 2 x 2 round plate.

To build the red and gray top, collect the bricks shown.

Attach all of the 2 x 2 round plates on the underside of the 4 x 4 round plate.

Build the top side as shown.

Try building a design with black and white.

The black and white design on this top creates a fun optical illusion when it's spinning.

BUILD A BRAIN TEASER PUZZLE

NO-INSTRUCTION CREATIVE CHALLENGE

Build a LEGO puzzle and challenge a friend to solve it! These simple puzzles fit together to create a square that is 10 studs by 10 studs. It's easy to build puzzle pieces that fit into a 10 x 10 square. But once the pieces are apart, can you get them back to a square again?

KEY ELEMENTS

Bricks in various colors
Plates in various colors

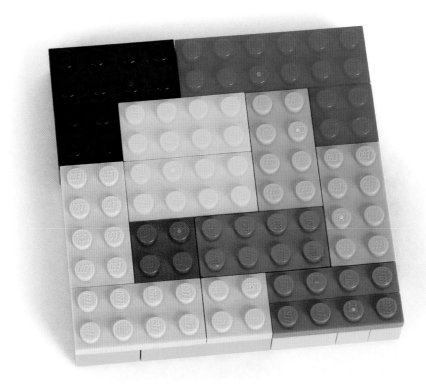

Use plates to hold bricks together in the shape of the pieces that you want. Try to make the top of each puzzle piece one solid color because it makes the puzzle easier to solve, but if you have to mix colors it's not a major problem.

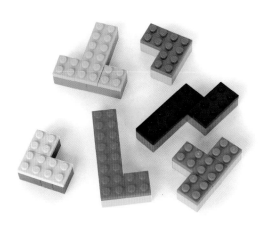

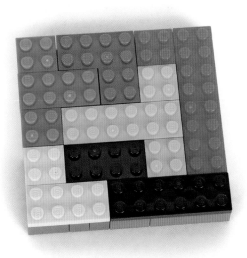

PUZZLE DESIGN #1: These pieces all fit into a square. Build them and try to solve the puzzle. Don't check the solution picture until you have given it a good try!

This photo shows the solution for Puzzle #1.

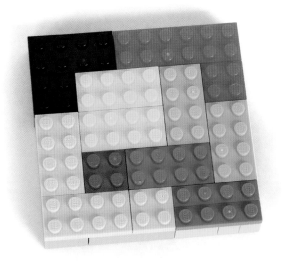

PUZZLE DESIGN #2. Here is another puzzle design with differently shaped pieces. The square makes it a challenge to solve!

This photo shows the solution for Puzzle #2.

Now try designing your own brain teaser puzzles!

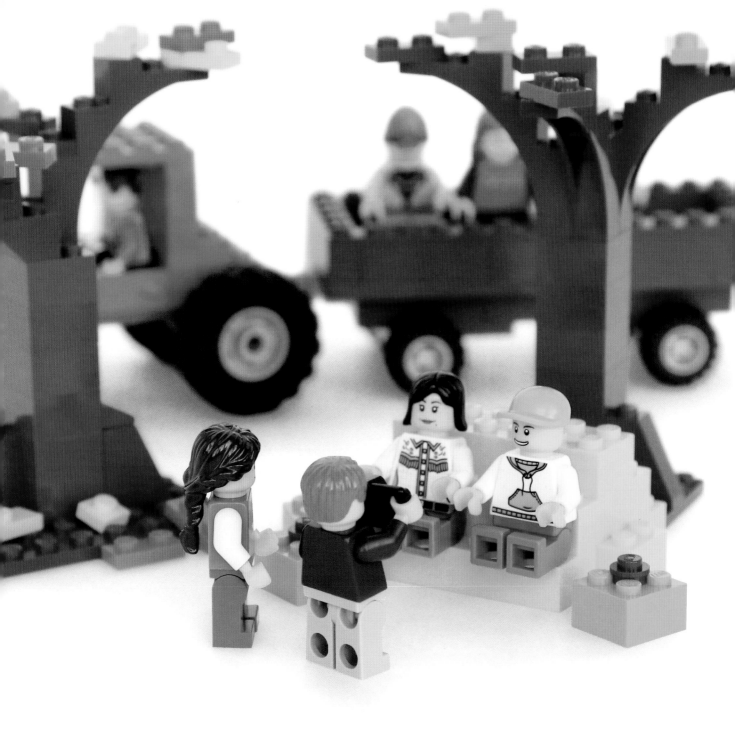

CHAPTER 8

LEGO ALL YEAR

No matter what season it is, there is something to be enjoyed or celebrated in each season of the year! Build an adorable LEGO snowman and create a minifigure snowball fight. When the weather gets warm in the summer, build a swimming pool and a snow cone stand. It's definitely a LEGO year!

SPRING
STEP-BY-STEP

Spring is a time when new life is appearing everywhere! It's always so wonderful after the cold winter weather to see the sun shining, new leaves appearing on the trees and new little animals. Celebrate spring by building some LEGO flowers, a rabbit and a basket full of colorful eggs.

PARTS LIST

TAN BRICKS
4—2 x 4 bricks
2—2 x 3 bricks
4—1 x 4 bricks
3—2 x 6 bricks
2—1 x 6 bricks
3—1 x 2 bricks
1—1 x 2 brick with two studs on the side
4—1 x 1 bricks with one stud on the side

6—2 x 4 plates
2—1 x 3 plates
4—1 x 2 plates
1—2 x 2 plate
2—1 x 1 plates
1—1 x 2 plate with one stud on the top
4—1 x 2 slopes
1—2 x 2 slope, inverted
2—1 x 3 curved slopes
3—1 x 2 slopes, 30 degree
2—1 x 1 slopes, 30 degree

WHITE BRICKS
1—4 x 6 plate
1—2 x 2 plate
1—2 x 2 brick
4—1 x 2 slopes with cutout
1—1 x 2 slope, 30 degree

ASSORTED BRICKS
1—1 x 1 pink round plate
2—eyes

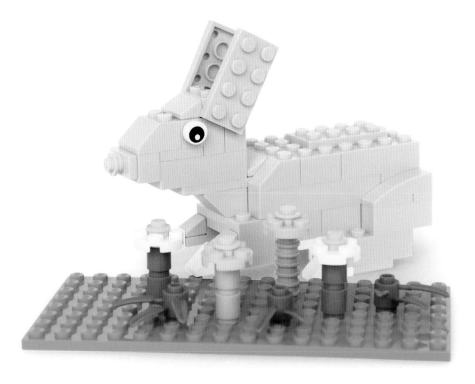

To build the flowers, use two 1 x 1 round bricks or several 1 x 1 round plates for the stem. The flower part is made up of a 2 x 2 round plate and a 1 x 1 round plate.

STEP 1: To build the rabbit, start with a white 4 x 6 plate for the body.

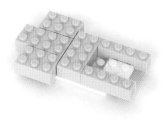

STEP 2: Add two 2 x 4 tan bricks, two 1 x 4 tan bricks and two 2 x 3 tan bricks. Place a 2 x 2 white plate in between the 1 x 4 tan bricks. The 1 x 4 bricks should hang off the white plate by two studs and the 2 x 2 white plate should hang off by 1 stud.

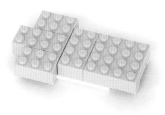

STEP 3: Stack two 2 x 4 tan plates and place them on top of the 2 x 2 white plate. This should create a flat layer of tan.

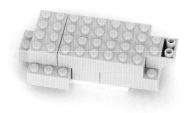

STEP 4: Add a tan 2 x 2 inverted slope, two 2 x 6 tan bricks and a 2 x 4 brick.

STEP 5: Add two 1 x 2 tan slopes and a layer of tan bricks as shown. Find two 2 x 4 tan plates and a tan 1 x 2 (30 degree) slope for the neck and back of the rabbit.

STEP 6: Add one 2 x 4 tan plate and the 1 x 2 tan slope to the neck. Place the other 2 x 4 tan plate on the back of the rabbit. Build the front legs as shown. Each front leg has a 1 x 3 tan plate, a 1 x 2 tan plate, a 1 x 1 tan slope and a 1 x 2 white slope with cutout.

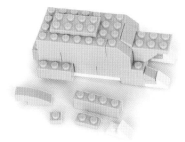

STEP 7: Gather the bricks shown for each back leg.

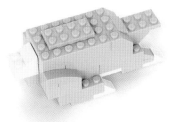

STEP 8: Attach a 1 x 1 tan plate and a 1 x 3 tan curved slope to the top of the brick that sticks out for each back leg. Add a 1 x 4 tan brick, a 1 x 2 tan plate and a white 1 x 2 slope with cutout underneath the brick that sticks out for each back leg.

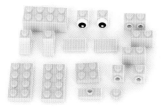

STEP 9: Gather the bricks shown for the rabbit's face.

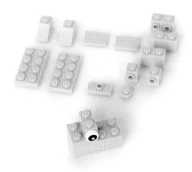

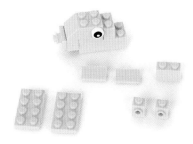

STEP 10: Start with a 2 x 4 tan brick. Add a 1 x 2 tan plate in the front and then two 1 x 1 tan bricks with a stud on the side. Add the eyes to these bricks.

STEP 11: Add two 1 x 2 tan slopes (or a 2 x 2 slope) in front of the eyes. Attach a 1 x 2 tan brick with two studs on the side to the underside of this slope brick.

STEP 12: Add a 1 x 2 tan plate with one stud on top and a pink nose as shown. Add a 1 x 2 tan brick behind the eyes.

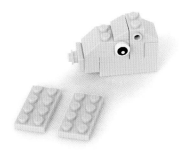

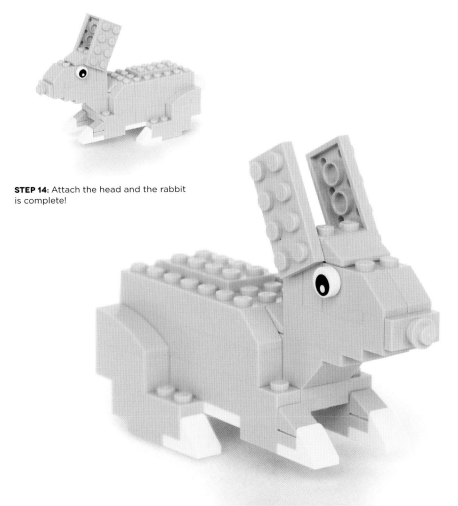

STEP 13: Complete the head as shown. The ears (2 x 4 plates) attach to the studs on the side of the head.

STEP 14: Attach the head and the rabbit is complete!

Use brown bricks to build a basket full of colorful eggs. Lime green 2 x 4 plates make the perfect grass for inside the basket. This basket has a layer of green plates inside the basket and then we used more 2 x 4 plates loose in the basket to look like grass.

Gather 2 x 4 bricks in bright colors to use as colored eggs.

SUMMER

NO-INSTRUCTION CREATIVE CHALLENGE

Summer is a time for playing in the sun, splashing in the pool and enjoying ice cold snow cones! Help your LEGO minifigures cool off on a hot day with this refreshing swimming pool. Then get them a treat at the LEGO snow cone stand.

KEY ELEMENTS

SWIMMING POOL

25—2 x 4 medium azure blue plates
Gray bricks for building the edge of the pool

PATIO CHAIRS

2—4 x 6 white plates
2—1 x 2 white plates with clips on the side
2—1 x 2 white plates with a handle on the side
2—2 x 4 medium azure blue plates
8—1 x 1 red bricks

PATIO TABLE WITH UMBRELLA

4—1 x 2 light gray bricks
1—4 x 6 dark gray plate
1—2 x 2 plate with one stud on top
1—2 x 2 round red plate
1—large disk
1—1 x 6 rod

To build the pool, arrange twenty-five 2 x 4 bright blue plates in rows of five. Or make the pool larger! Add details like plants, patio furniture and accessories for the minifigures.

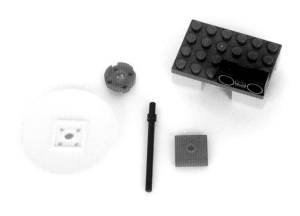

The patio chairs are very simple to put together. Make the back of the chair adjustable by attaching a 1 x 2 plate with a handle and a 1 x 2 plate with clips.

These are the bricks needed for the patio table and umbrella. The legs of the table are four 1 x 2 light gray bricks.

Stick the rod through the hole in the large disk. Then add a 2 x 2 round plate to secure it in place.

The completed table should look like this.

Try building your minifigures a snow cone stand! Build the syrup dispensers by using 1 x 1 bricks in different colors and then putting a nozzle on top. Each snow cone is a 1 x 1 round white brick with a translucent 1 x 1 round plate on top.

The LEGO snow cone stand is a great place to hang out in the summer! But wow, those must be some expensive snow cones! Either that or the kids are going to get a lot of change back. What flavors will you build for your snow cone stand?

FALL
STEP-BY-STEP

After the heat of summer, there is so much to love about fall! Fall brings cooler weather, colorful leaves and pumpkins. Build a pumpkin patch for your mini figures, complete with a hay ride. Look, even the minifigure parents are making their kids pose for photos with the pumpkins!

PARTS LIST

BLUE BRICKS
3—2 x 4 bricks
1—1 x 4 brick
4—1 x 1 bricks
4—2 x 4 plates
3—1 x 4 plates
1—1 x 2 plate
1—4 x 4 plate
2—car doors

DARK GRAY BRICKS
1—4 x 10 plate
1—4 x 4 plate
1—1 x 4 tile
1—1 x 2 brick with ridges

LIGHT GRAY BRICKS
2—1 x 1 bricks with a stud on the side
2—2 x 4 bricks with axles
2—1 x 1 plates
1—2 x 2 plate with a ball
1—1 x 4 plate with a socket on the side
4—2 x 2 plates with one axle

BROWN BRICKS
8—1 x 4 bricks
2—1 x 2 bricks
6—2 x 4 bricks
1—6 x 12 plate
1—2 x 6 plate
2—4 x 4 plates
4—1 x 4 plates

2—1 x 2 plates
1—1 x 6 plate
1—1 x 10 plate
1 x 1 round plates for the pumpkins

ASSORTED BRICKS
2—1 x 1 yellow round plates
2 x 2 orange bricks for the pumpkins
4—small wheels
2—large wheels
2—medium wheels
1—windshield
1—steering wheel
Various yellow plates for the hay
Various bricks for the trees

The kids are tired of sitting still for photos, but Dad wants to get just one more shot!

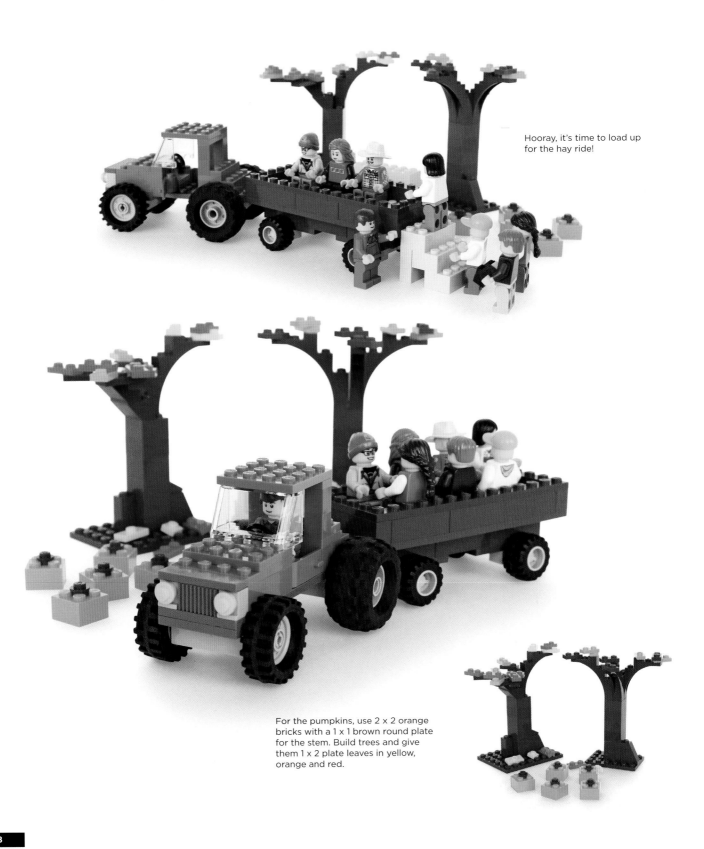

Hooray, it's time to load up for the hay ride!

For the pumpkins, use 2 x 2 orange bricks with a 1 x 1 brown round plate for the stem. Build trees and give them 1 x 2 plate leaves in yellow, orange and red.

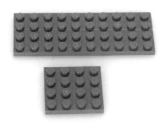

STEP 1: To build the tractor, find a 4 x 10 dark gray plate and a 4 x 4 dark gray plate.

STEP 2: Attach the 4 x 4 dark gray plate under the larger plate on one end. This will be the front end of the tractor.

STEP 3: Build the front of the tractor as shown.

STEP 4: Add three 2 x 4 blue plates and a 1 x 4 blue plate to the front of the truck. Add the doors. Place a 1 x 2 blue plate under the steering wheel to boost it up to the proper height.

STEP 5: Attach the 2 x 2 light gray plate with a tow ball and two 1 x 1 light gray plates to the back wheel axle as shown.

STEP 6: Attach the wheels to the body of the tractor. The back axle will only attach to the body with one row of studs.

STEP 7: Add a 2 x 4 blue brick and a 1 x 4 blue brick behind the doors.

STEP 8: Build the roof for the tractor. The back of the cab has two 1 x 1 blue bricks on each side, a 1 x 4 blue plate across them and then a 4 x 4 blue plate for the roof.

STEP 9: Add the headlights and a 1 x 4 dark gray tile at the front of the truck and the tractor is finished!

STEP 10: Build the wagon. Start with a 6 x 12 brown plate and a 2 x 6 brown plate.

STEP 11: Add one row of brown bricks and one row of brown plates to the perimeter of the wagon.

STEP 12: Turn the wagon upside down. Add six 2 x 4 brown bricks, two 4 x 4 brown plates and one 1 x 4 light gray plate with a tow ball socket as shown.

STEP 13: Add the wheels.

STEP 14: Use yellow plates to look like hay inside the wagon, and the tractor and wagon are complete!

WINTER

NO-INSTRUCTION CREATIVE CHALLENGE

The weather outside might be dreadful, but what better time to be creative with LEGO inside? Beat the winter blues with a LEGO snowball fight and a snowman. Try building your minifigures some skis. Use some white slope bricks to create a hill to ski down. Maybe you can figure out how to build a sled!

PARTS LIST

Various brown bricks and plates to build a tree

Various white bricks for the snow fort
1 x 1 white round plates for snow balls
2—1 x 6 plates for the skis

2—1 x 1 slopes, 30 degree, for the skis
2—Technic pins (flick missile style) for the ski poles

Use 1 x 1 round white plates as snowballs. The minifigures will be able to hold them attached to their hands.

Use a large white plate to build a snow fort. Build up the walls of the fort with white bricks and white sloped bricks.

For the skis, use 1 x 6 plates and 1 x 1 (30 degree) slope bricks. Technic connector pins make great ski poles.

A little cross-country skiing is a great activity for a winter day!

SNOWMAN
STEP-BY-STEP

Build a snowman for your winter scene! This snowman is a good size to go with minifigures.

PARTS LIST

WHITE BRICKS

2—2 x 4 slopes, double inverted
3—2 x 2 slopes, inverted
2—2 x 2 slopes
2—1 x 2 slopes, 30 degree
1—2 x 4 brick
4—1 x 2 bricks
4—1 x 1 bricks with a stud on the side

1—1 x 4 plate
5—1 x 2 plates
3—1 x 2 plates with one stud on top
2—1 x 1 plates

RED BRICKS

1—1 x 2 brick
1—2 x 2 x ⅔ high brick, modified with
   curved end

BROWN BRICKS

2—1 x 3 plates
2—1 x 2 plates

BLACK BRICKS

2—1 x 1 round plates

ORANGE BRICKS

1—orange claw for the nose

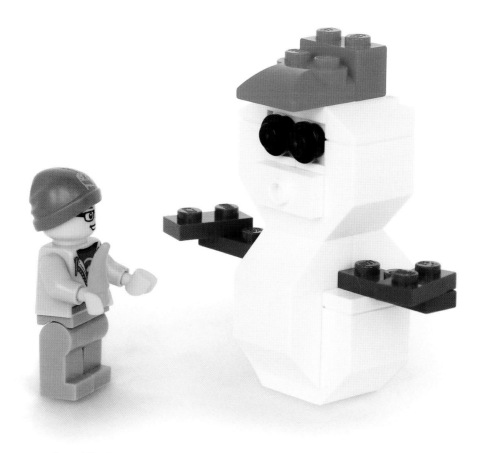

It would be fun to watch your minifigures add the snowman's finishing touches!

STEP 1: Use a white double inverted slope as the base for the snowman.

STEP 2: Add two white 2 x 2 inverted slope bricks.

STEP 3: In this step, add a 2 x 4 white brick, two 1 x 2 white bricks and two 1 x 2 white plates with one stud on top. These will hold the snowman's arms.

STEP 4: Add two 2 x 2 white slope bricks to the body. On top of that, add another double inverted slope and a white 2 x 2 inverted slope.

STEP 5: Add two 1 x 1 white bricks with a stud on the side. Then add two more on top of those. Attach a 1 x 2 white plate with a stud on top to the bottom set of bricks. Attach the eyes (black 1 x 1 round plates) to the top set of bricks.

STEP 6: In this step, add two 1 x 2 white plates, a 1 x 4 white plate and a 1 x 2 white brick.

STEP 7: Add two 1 x 1 white plates on the side of the head. Then add two 1 x 2 white plates and two white 1 x 2 slopes on the sides of the head. Place a 1 x 2 white plate above the eyes. Fill in the hole in the head with a 1 x 2 white brick. Then gather the bricks shown to build the hat and arms.

The snowman is complete!

CLASSIC CHRISTMAS TREE SCENE

NO-INSTRUCTION CREATIVE CHALLENGE

The LEGO minifigures are celebrating a cozy Christmas with their own fireplace, Christmas tree and gifts. The scene also shows the living room chair, end table and lamp from the furniture project in the LEGO Town chapter (pages 100–101). What do you think could be inside that huge present?

KEY ELEMENTS

FIREPLACE
2—2 x 2 brown slopes, inverted
1—2 x 8 brown plate
2—1 x 2 brown tiles
Various light gray bricks

1—1 x 2 light gray Technic brick
1—Technic pin ½ length
6—2 x 2 green corner plates
4—1 x 1 red round plates

CHRISTMAS TREE
1—4 x 4 tan plate

3—2 x 2 brown round plates
Red and white 1 x 1 round plates
Green 1 x 2 bricks, 2 x 4 plates, 2 x 2 plates and 2 x 2 corner plates
1—1 x 1 yellow round plate
1—1 x 1 yellow plate

The anticipation is almost as fun as playing with whatever is in the box. Right?

He has the lid off, but what could be in there?

It's a puppy! What fun to find a puppy under the tree!

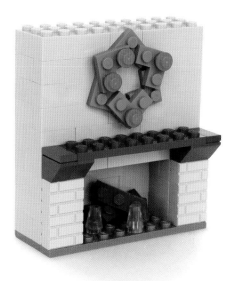

Build the fireplace with gray bricks, using brown inverted slopes to hold up the mantle. Build the wreath with six 2 x 2 green corner plates. Decorate it with 1 x 1 red round plates. The wreath hangs on the fireplace with a 1 x 2 Technic brick and a Technic pin (half length).

Use 1 x 1 translucent orange cones and 1 x 3 brown plates to make it look like there is a fire in the fireplace.

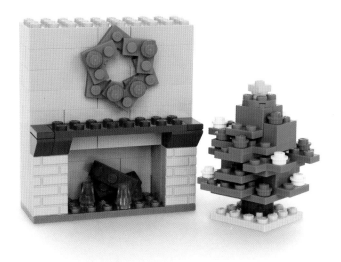

The trunk of the Christmas tree is three 2 x 2 brown round plates or you can also use a 2 x 2 brown round brick. Create your tree with the green bricks that you have on hand and use 1 x 1 green and white round plates to decorate the tree. Or use other colors as well for a more colorful tree!

The tree is trimmed and the fire is blazing! Now you can place LEGO gifts under the tree! Basic 2 x 4 and 2 x 2 bricks work well for gifts. Add tiles or 1 x 1 round plates as bows.

SANTA
STEP-BY-STEP

This jolly large-scale Santa is attractive enough to display on the fireplace mantle during the Christmas season. His friendly eyes and rosy cheeks give him plenty of Christmas spirit. The parts list for this project can be flexible. Once you have built the head, there are many possible combinations of red and white bricks that can be used for the body and legs.

PARTS LIST

RED BRICKS
1—2 x 2 plate
1—2 x 4 plate
2—1 x 4 plates
2—2 x 6 plates
1—2 x 8 plate
5—2 x 4 bricks
5—2 x 8 bricks
4—1 x 2 bricks
8—2 x 2 bricks
10—2 x 3 bricks
1—2 x 4 slope
2—2 x 3 bricks with a rounded end
2—1 x 3 tiles
1—2 x 4 slope, lengthwise
2—1 x 2 slopes, 30 degree
4—2 x 2 slopes, 2 bricks high
1—bracket 1 x 2—2 x 2

BLACK BRICKS
3—2 x 6 plates
2—2 x 3 plates
1—2 x 2 plate
1—2 x 4 plate
2—2 x 4 bricks
4—1 x 2 bricks
1—bracket 1 x 2—2 x 2
2—1 x 2 slopes, 30 degree

WHITE BRICKS
1—1 x 4 plate
1—1 x 2 plate
1—2 x 6 plate
1—1 x 6 plate
2—1 x 3 plates
2—2 x 2 plates
2—2 x 4 bricks
4—1 x 3 bricks
3—1 x 2 bricks

2—1 x 1 bricks
2—2 x 6 bricks
3—1 x 4 bricks
4—2 x 2 slopes, inverted
2—1 x 2 slopes, inverted
1—1 x 4 tile

TAN BRICKS
1—2 x 4 plate
2—2 x 2 plates
2—1 x 3 bricks
2—1 x 2 bricks
2—2 x 4 bricks
4—1 x 1 bricks with a stud on the side
1—2 x 2 slope

ASSORTED BRICKS
2—eyes
2—1 x 1 pink round plates

STEP 1: Begin Santa's head with a 2 x 4 tan plate.

STEP 2: Add a 2 x 2 red plate, two 2 x 2 tan plates and two 1 x 3 tan bricks.

STEP 3: Add a 2 x 2 tan slope for the nose, a 1 x 2 tan brick and four 1 x 1 tan bricks with a stud on the side. These will hold the eyes and two 1 x 1 pink round plates for the rosy cheeks.

STEP 4: Build Santa's mustache with a 1 x 4 white plate and a 1 x 2 white plate. Add two tan 2 x 4 bricks to the head behind the nose and eyes.

STEP 5: Fill in the gap in Santa's head with a 1 x 2 tan brick.

STEP 6: Start on the hat with a 2 x 6 white plate, a 1 x 6 white plate and a 2 x 4 red plate.

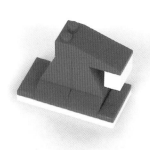

STEP 7: Add two red 2 x 2 slopes (2 bricks high), a red 2 x 4 slope, a 1 x 2 white brick, two 1 x 3 tiles and two 1 x 2 red slopes (30 degree) to the hat.

STEP 8: Build the sides of Santa's beard as shown. Then gather a white 2 x 4 brick and two white 2 x 2 inverted slopes for the bottom of the beard.

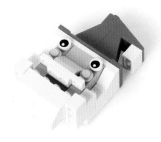

STEP 9: Attach the 2 x 4 white brick and the two white 2 x 2 inverted slopes to the underside of the face as shown.

STEP 10: Arrange white bricks as shown for the bottom of Santa's coat.

STEP 11: Add a layer of red bricks and two layers of black plates as shown. Place a black bracket in the center (1 x 2—2 x 2) for Santa's belt.

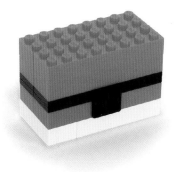

STEP 12: Add two more layers of red bricks.

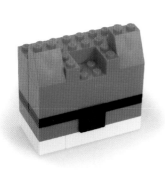

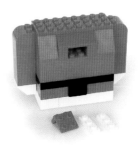

STEP 13: Add two 1 x 2 red bricks and two red 2 x 2 slopes (2 bricks high) to the front row. Add a 2 x 8 red brick (or the equivalent) to the back row.

STEP 14: Add two 2 x 3 red bricks with curved ends as Santa's shoulders. Add two 1 x 2 bricks and a 2 x 4 red brick to the back row. Add a 2 x 4 red slope brick to the front of his body. Build the arms. Each arm has four 2 x 2 red bricks and a 2 x 2 white inverted slope.

STEP 15: Attach Santa's arms to his body. Add a 2 x 8 red plate and two 1 x 4 red plates on top of the body. Then gather the bricks shown.

STEP 16: Add a 1 x 2—2 x 2 red bracket to the top of the opening in the body. This will hold the white trim for Santa's suit.

STEP 17: Attach the white trim. Stack two 2 x 6 red plates and add them to the neck. Place two 2 x 2 white plates on top of that.

STEP 18: Attach Santa's head to his body. Then gather three 1 x 4 white bricks and one 1 x 4 white tile for his hair.

STEP 19: Build Santa's hair as shown.

STEP 20: Build the legs and feet and add them to the body. Each leg is five 2 x 3 red bricks. Each shoe is one 2 x 4 black brick, two 1 x 2 black bricks and one 1 x 2 slope. Santa is now ready to display!

OUTTAKES

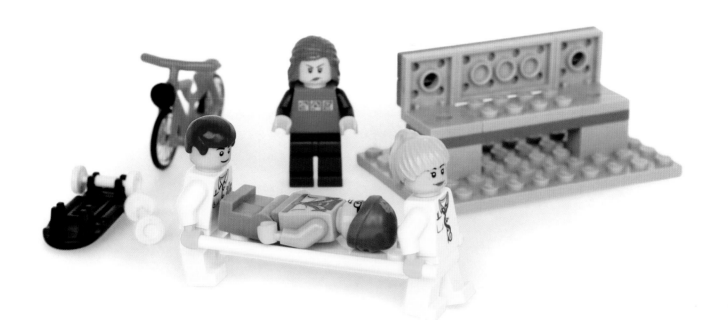

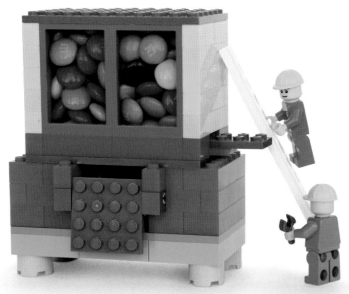

ACKNOWLEDGMENTS

Thank you to everyone at Page Street Publishing Company for making this LEGO book come to life!

Writing this book was truly a family endeavor and I am so thankful to my husband Jordan and my boys Aidan, Gresham, Owen and Jonathan for helping to design and test the projects in this book. I could not have done it without you! Thank you also to our toddler daughter, Janie, who put up with a busy family and constant requests to please not take apart the LEGO projects. You'll be old enough to join in next time!

A huge thank you to my husband, my mom and Angela Speers for providing child care so that I could edit photos and write LEGO instructions. Rachel Miller and Asia Citro, thank you for all of the support and the advice that you provided about the book writing process!

Thank you to Heidi Sears for providing help with the photography and photo editing (your tips saved the day!) and thank you to all of the Sears boys for your ideas and input. Thank you to Becki Miller and Matthew for editing the manuscript and providing input.

And finally, thank you to all of our loyal Frugal Fun for Boys readers for your encouragement and support!

ABOUT
THE AUTHOR

Sarah Dees is an educator, wife to her wonderful husband, Jordan, and a busy mom of five LEGO-loving kids. She enjoys learning and exploring the outdoors with her kids, as well as creating all kinds of neat LEGO projects. It's not unusual for her playroom floor to be covered with LEGO bricks—with the whole family building! Her blog, Frugal Fun for Boys, is packed full of crafts, activities and games that boys will go for, but it's definitely not for boys only! Check out her latest projects, including LEGO ideas, at frugalfun4boys.com.

INDEX